The Seven Letters
A Secret Guide to Everyday Life

Volume 1

Kristina Kaine

Cover: St John the Evangelist by Carlo Dolci

Cover designed by Adriana Koulias, with heartfelt thanks for her creative and generous spirit.

Copyright © 2020 Kristina Kaine

All rights reserved.

ISBN: 9780992416843

DEDICATION

I dedicated this book to all those who devotedly seek to understand the spiritual aspect behind all life.

I also dedicate this book to St John the Baptist.

I began writing these Reflections on St John's Day, June 24 2019 and the last Reflection in this book was written in the week following St John's Day, June 28 2020.

The Seven Letters were written by Disciples who experienced the reality of the Christen-ed Jesus personally. These letters consist of James, 1 and 2 Peter, 1, 2, and 3 John, and Jude. They are often called the General (or Catholic) Epistles because they to speak to us rather than to the church in general. They are a guide explaining how our consciousness will change as we awaken the resurrected presence of Christ within us. The Revised Standard Version of the Bible has been used.

"We are not at all I -
but we can and shall become I.
We are seeds for becoming I.
We shall all transform into a you -
into a second I -
only thereby do we raise ourselves to the Great I -
which is One and All together."
Friedrich von Hardenberg (Novalis) 1772-1801.

CONTENTS

	Acknowledgments	i
1	James 1	1
2	James 2	27
3	James 3	42
4	James 4	51
5	James 5	63
6	1 Peter 1	79
7	1 Peter 2	96
8	1 Peter 3	113
9	1 Peter 4	127
10	1 Peter 5	141

ACKNOWLEDGMENTS

Thank you to all my dear friends who inspired this work. Your generosity of spirit fills me with warmth and nourishment. My deepest wish is that we can all support each other in this way.

To see the light in another person, no matter how dim, causes that light to flicker and generate its own energy. This is the greatest gift one human being can give another.

CHAPTER 1
THE LETTER OF JAMES
JAMES 1

Towards the end of the Bible, between the Book of Hebrews and The Revelation, are Seven Letters. They are written by James, John, Peter and Jude. These letters are short and they are written to us, the people who are endeavoring to integrate a radically new consciousness, not just on the earth but in the whole Universe. Since the crucifixion and resurrection of Christ on the earth this Universe was so radically changed that not even the Gods were able to participate as they used to, and so they withdrew.

These were the Gods that guided the human race down the centuries until the time Jesus was born. Humanity depended on them for everything. Now, with the deed of Christ, humanity was left to their own resources. This is a great responsibility and it is up to each individual to discover their path. No longer led and guided by others, but, with an understanding of what lies ahead, stepping out with self-confidence.

Even today, this is not a fully acceptable idea. We are always encouraged to follow a leader. The one who claims to be the leader has often placed themselves in this position through manipulating situations to benefit themselves. If anyone speaks out they will be suppressed in various ways. This is a long way from where we need to be.

Our goal, and the purpose of the Christ-Jesus event on the earth, is to reveal the god within every person. This spiritual being within each of us is now working towards self-realization and the recognition of the highest in every other person. Then, to find ways to work in community while acknowledging the individuality in each one.

This work is part of everyday life. It can be as simple as being aware of how we entice others to agree with our ideas, which usually means we do not value their ideas. We see this coercion everywhere in life. At its core is the fear of standing alone in our individuality.

The Seven Letters, as we will discover, reveal the stages of our journey. It is interesting that there are seven letters, just as there are many groups of seven in the Bible, and especially in The Revelation, which also includes seven letters.

The first of the seven letters is written by James. We can't know who James is for sure; he could be Jesus' half-brother or another follower of Jesus. To explore this would take us on an exoteric journey when the journey we are taking is the esoteric journey. This esoteric journey will inform us of the changes taking place in the Universe, and in us, as the being of Christ integrates into human life - then and now.

James, a servant of God and of the Lord Jesus Christ, To the twelve tribes in the Dispersion: Greeting. Count it all joy, my brethren, when you meet various trials, for you know that the testing of your faith produces steadfastness. And let steadfastness have its full effect, that you may be perfect and complete, lacking in nothing. James 1:1-4

We know deep down that we long to be perfect and complete. We also know that we always feel a long way off from this goal. It is like an inner incentive to strive to be better while knowing that we will never fully reach that goal, we always have more to do, greater things to achieve. We can never be satisfied with ourselves. If we do, we can be assured that some being is whispering in our consciousness to distract us from our work.

If we look at the original meaning of some of the words in this text a different story emerges. The name James is translated from the Hebrew name Jacob which means "heel holder" or "supplanter". Jacob in the Old Testament is the son of Isaac, grandson of Abraham, and father of the 12 patriarchs of the tribes of Israel. This would indicate that the original principals that guided humankind along its journey are speaking to us again through James after the Christ event that Abraham prepared the way for.

James calls himself a servant, *doulos*, which means the one who freely gives himself up to another's will. This is when we don't fight for our ideas but let the other person express their ideas. The tendency to shut down what others say when we think they disagree with us is common. We give ourselves to them if we hold our own ideas and find ways to integrate their ideas. This collaboration can bring both parties to a higher understanding.

The twelve tribes can be seen as the twelve mind faculties which are now part of the dispersion, the *diaspora*, meaning to scatter or spread about. They are no longer directed by the Gods but now each person takes responsibility for their expression.

Each word in the text has several meanings, one is the external everyday meaning, the other is the inner power of the word. "Greeting" is the word *chairo* which means rejoice. "Count it all joy" where the word 'count' is *hegeomai* which means to lead or be a leader. This really means to lead by example. To show others how to be the individual they now need to be if the power of Christ is to be awakened in each one of us.

> *James, a servant of God and of the Lord Jesus Christ, To the twelve tribes in the Dispersion: Greeting. Count it all joy, my brethren, when you meet various trials, for you know that the testing of your faith produces steadfastness. And let steadfastness have its full effect, that you may be perfect and complete, lacking in nothing. James 1:1-4*

When we explore the meaning of the Greek words translated into English in the Bible, we find deeper, broader meanings. This is the case with any language; however it is more difficult with a language like Koine or Biblical Greek which was spoken over 2,000 years ago. Hidden within these texts are many deeper meanings which are only revealed to those who dedicate themselves to unraveling them.

Here is one way to re-express the first verse.

James, the supplanter, is replacing or 'filling a place' once occupied by something that is no longer adequate. As a servant, *doulos*, he is giving himself up to the will of God and the Lord Jesus Christ. This giving up of one's self is not mindless subservience; it is done with full conscious awareness. It does not involve bondage, there is equality about it, and we find this equality in the I Am, the *ego eimi*, the Higher Self.

From this position James is writing to "the twelve tribes in the Dispersion". James gives us a sense of what is taking place when he mentions the Dispersion, the *diaspora,* the scattering. This speaks of individuals moving away from a state where they were led by elders, and taking responsibility for themselves and their own work in the world.

We can apply this idea to what takes place within us as our consciousness evolves, then the twelve tribes can be seen as the twelve mind faculties. These faculties were also represented by the twelve disciples.

Andrew	Inner strength and humility
Simon Peter	Hearing and faith
Phillip	Power
Nathanael Bartholomew	Imagination
Judas	Generative forces
Thomas	Understanding
John	Love
Thaddaeus	Renunciation and elimination
Matthew	Will, the tax collector
James the son of Alphaeus	Order
James the son of Zeb'edee	Discrimination or Judgement
Simon the Cananaean	Zeal, enthusiasm

From "I Am the Soul's Heartbeat Volume 4" by Kristina Kaine

Then James says, "Greeting", this is not a simple "Hello". This is a deep recognition and respect for what is taking place in others. The Greek word for greeting is *chairo* and it means joy and rejoice - it is signaling a celebration. "Greeting. Count it all joy, my brethren" speaks to us of a new level of cooperation between those who are awakening to the presence of Christ within and around them since the crucifixion on Golgotha. They have been reborn and James calls them brethren, *adelphos,* meaning they come from the same womb - in this case the womb of Christ.

The word 'count', *hegeomai,* means to lead or be a leader, and points to the way in which each individual demonstrates that they are walking this new path. No longer is it about saying we obey the law, now the inner law expresses itself in everything we do, in every thought and feeling that guides our behavior. This is especially important when we "meet various trials". The word 'meet' is *peripipto* which means to descend from a higher place to a lower. Trials can only be met in a lower place.

This explains that we can't rise up to our Higher Self and ignore what takes place below. We live on this earth for a reason; we have descended from the spiritual worlds to become self-realized individuals. We see this same modus operandi in the descent of Christ into the body of Jesus.

Trials, *peirasmos,* describe an experiment, a proving. This is exactly what we do; we prove that we are capable of living on this earth while engaging with the influence of the Higher Self. Jesus showed us how to do this; he was fully engaged with earthly life as he, over three years, took into himself the highest, the Christ Spirit.

In verse 3 we read, "for you know that the testing of your faith produces steadfastness."

Know, *ginosko*, means to fully enter into a thing. *Ginosko* is the Jewish idiom for sexual intercourse. Testing, *dokimion*, speaks of the proof, the acceptable evidence not just the activity of testing itself. Faith *pistis*, doesn't mean to believe blindly, it speaks of the experience of *ginosko*, of fully entering into the matter. Steadfastness, *hypomone,* indicates patient endurance and it has a sense of waiting while knowing what we are waiting for.

We get a sense of a real experience, a life-changing experience, rather than a theory to be unraveled. If we could go back to the society at the time of Christ we would probably understand what a massive change was taking place within those who were experiencing the deed of Christ as a reality in their lives.

In verse 4 the presence of the I Am is suggested in the

words 'have' *echo* and 'be' *eimi*.

"And let steadfastness have its full effect, that you may be perfect and complete, lacking in nothing."

Have, *echo,* means to possess one's self - and points to possessing the Higher Self. "Perfect and complete" is not a good translation. The Greek words are *"Telios ergon"* where *teleios* means the full effect and *ergon* means work. Again suggesting that we need to make complete effort and then nothing will be lacking, *leipo,* which means leave behind. So we will leave nothing behind which is an important point because often when actions are taken there are leftover effects.

If any of you lacks wisdom, let him ask God, who gives to all men generously and without reproaching, and it will be given him. But let him ask in faith, with no doubting, for he who doubts is like a wave of the sea that is driven and tossed by the wind. For that person must not suppose that a double-minded man, unstable in all his ways, will receive anything from the Lord. James 1:5-8

Reading this text superficially we are given a sense of the power of God in the light of our own powerlessness. We could think that we are being asked to give in, and give up our will, to a mighty being not fully known to us. Yet, what takes place in us when we remove doubting? Our will becomes active. We don't simply push doubting away blindly, we explore inner meanings, which is what we are doing by exploring the words in this sacred text in the hope of moving from doubting to knowing. This is the purpose of all sacred writing; it holds the truth securely only to reveal it to those who dedicate themselves to seeking it.

Verse five begins with a mighty statement, "If any of you

lacks wisdom" which in the original language says, "If any of you leaves behind Sophia". The word 'lacks' is *eipo* which primarily means to leave, leave behind, or forsake. The word 'wisdom' is *Sophia*.

In his lectures on The Gospel of St John, Rudolf Steiner describes Sophia in this way.

"This cleansed, purified astral body, which bears within it at the moment of illumination none of the impure impressions of the physical world, but only the organs of perception of the spiritual world, is called in esoteric Christianity the "pure, chaste, wise Virgin Sophia." Lecture 12 May 31, 1908

In the Bible we find Sophia in Mary, the mother of Jesus, specifically the mother of the Luke Jesus.

You will conceive and give birth to a son, and you are to call him Jesus. He will be great and will be called the Son of the Most High. [...] "How will this be," Mary asked the angel, "since I am a virgin?" Luke 1:31,32,34

Does Sophia have a place in our life? Or have we left her behind? In sacred texts every detail matters. We can't simply focus on Jesus and ignore all the other characters just as we can't focus on our physical body and ignore our etheric, astral and 'I' bodies. Unless we become part of Sophia we cannot give birth to Christ.

We can put this quite simply by saying that if we cleanse our astral body, by purifying our feeling, thinking, and will in our soul, we enable our soul, Sophia, to give birth to Jesus, our I Am, facilitating the entrance of the living Christ into our soul. This reveals to us all the elements we must work on if we are to have wisdom and develop organs of perception. In his book "The Most Holy Trinosophia" Robert Powell reveals many details about the place of Sophia, the "Divine Feminine" in our lives. He says, "a true knowledge of this being is vital for a meaningful understanding of the Second Coming of Christ."

James tells us that if we have left Sophia behind, there is a way to find her. He says;

"let him ask God, who gives to all men generously and without reproaching, and it will be given him."

The inner meaning of some of these words gives us a greater understanding of what we can do to restore our relationship with Sophia. First we must ask. Ask in Greek is *aiteo* which means to desire and ask of someone in a higher position. Our desires have their home in our astral body, and the 'one' in a higher position is our soul where our desires are purified.

James says to ask God, *theos,* which is a general name of deities or divinities. These divinities are all the higher beings in the Cosmos from Angels to Cherubim (see my book "Bible Unlocked" for more detail about these beings). We can ask these beings out of a confident knowing that they are with us, surrounding us on this earth, as they guide all the conditions of the Universe to make life on earth possible for us.

How often do we think of the activity of these beings during the day? When we are able to factor them into our thoughts we draw on the wisdom that is Sophia. These beings then give generously: give is *didomi,* and speaks of adding something, producing something. This adding or producing is directly related to our ability to acknowledge their activity. *Haplos* is the word used for generously, but rather than generously it means simply, openly, sincerely. This adds to the sense of working together with these higher beings where something is exchanged according to the contribution we each make. There will be no reproach, *oneidizo,* which means blame or criticism. This tells us that we have no need to hide our flaws that are now revealed to our heightened spiritual insight.

The next verse is straightforward, *"But let him ask in faith, with no doubting, for he who doubts is like a wave of the sea that is driven and tossed by the wind."*

Faith *pistis*, means knowing, and 'without doubting' is *diakrino: dia* means through and *krino* means to separate out, to judge, to contend, to differ, which speaks of rebalancing - and doing it continually as each new piece of truth is understood. Truth, *alethes*, is the process of unforgetting and it is a continual inner process. Each new aspect of truth shines a light on the greater truth.

Let the lowly brother boast in his exaltation, and the rich in his humiliation, because like the flower of the grass he will pass away. For the sun rises with its scorching heat and withers the grass; its flower falls, and its beauty perishes. So will the rich man fade away in the midst of his pursuits. Blessed is the man who endures trial, for when he has stood the test he will receive the crown of life which God has promised to those who love him. James 1:9-12

The principal reason we explore sacred writings is to discover truth. The essential motivation for this is to understand ourselves, to discover who we really are. As long as we do not understand ourselves and the purpose of our life, we will experience some form of discontent. One of the ways we can identify the presence of discontent is by looking at a person's position in life. Are they rich or poor, and what is their attitude to being rich or poor; a poor person can seek sympathy, and a rich person can seek accolades. We see this process of over- or underestimating everywhere.

The key to understanding this passage can be found in the word for 'pursuits' which is *poreia* and means journey. We will never discover the truth about ourselves unless we understand the journey we are on. This journey involves living repeated lives on this earth, as well as repeated sojourns in the spiritual worlds between these lives. Not being able to remember this is like not being able to remember what we did yesterday or the day before, or what took place while we slept. In this way life is lived isolated from the truth of who we really are.

James is trying to give us an idea of how we might begin to live into this truth by using the analogy of the flowering grass. James, as the meaning of his name suggests, is showing us how to replace our empty ideas with an understanding of truth. The idea that the flowering grass will pass away suggests that we should not boast, *kauchaomai*, which also means rejoice, about the way we flower. The flower is simply a part of a much larger cycle. In fact, every time we see a plant shooting, budding or flowering we can compare it to the life cycles of our repeated lives. We can even apply the words 'pass away' to the idea of repeated lives. 'Pass away' is *parerchomai* where *parer* means coming or going, and e*rchomai* means to come from one place to another.

Each life we live on this earth is influenced by our activity in past lives which we call karma. It is only by considering karma that we can understand why one man is poor and another is rich. James is telling us to rejoice for a brother who is humble, *tapeinos*, in his height *hypsos,* and the rich man who humbles himself. This is not what happens in life however. The 'lowly brother' can seek sympathy for his situation and the 'rich man' can elevate his importance, which is nothing more than the lower ego at work.

If we apply this to knowledge rather than financial wealth we get an even better idea of the situation. Those who truly understand esoteric truth will often be understated. Those who have just begun to get a glimpse of this truth can throw their 'wealth' around.

We might ask why James is entering into this situation at the beginning of his Letter. This surely indicates the importance of the topic. James has had some insight into the purpose of the incarnation of Jesus, who was probably his half-brother. This insight revealed the entrance of the I Am into each human being. He has seen how the group I Am held by Jehovah is transitioning into each individual human being as described in the story of Pentecost where the individual flames entered into each person present.

Now James is describing the need for each human being to take personal responsibility for the use their will. One of the best ways to do this is to understand the esoteric nature of the will. It is a mysterious force deep within human nature. We are hardly conscious of it. When we start to become conscious of it through our studies, we should not boast about our success, instead we use our will to keep ourselves humble.

Through the will we can have the impulse to grab everything for ourselves. Animals do this; it is part of their nature. But as human beings we must rise above this inclination which lives in our astral. This even applies to our urge to always be right, to have the richest ideas. Yet, those who truly have the richest ideas are often the most humble. This is our trial now as James points out.

"Blessed is the man who endures trial, for when he has stood the test he will receive the crown of life which God has promised to those who love him."

The word trial is *peirasmos* which means to try whether a thing can be done - to endeavor. This also speaks to us of the use of our will. If we genuinely apply our will to quietening the impulse of the ego so that our I Am can take its rightful place in our soul we will endure the trial. Then we will receive the crown of life. There are several words meaning life in the Bible, the word used here is *zoe* which means spiritualized life-force or I Am infused etheric. This is part of the process of learning how to have personal use of our I Am, the gift of the incarnation of Christ, "which God has promised to those who love him." Of the four or more Greek words for love, this one is *agapao*, the highest love.

> *Let no one say when he is tempted, "I am tempted by God"; for God cannot be tempted with evil and he himself tempts no one; but each person is tempted when he is lured and enticed by his own desire. Then desire when it has conceived gives birth to sin; and sin when it is full-grown brings forth death. James 1:13-15*

To fully understand the meaning of words we have to go beyond their contemporary usage. The word 'tempted' is a good example. Tempted in Greek is *peirazo*, which essentially means to try whether a thing can be done. Therefore it is associated with the word attempt, to endeavor, which comes from the base word *pirah* meaning 'through the idea of piercing'. Furthermore, *pirah* comes from the base *peran* which means beyond, on the other side.

In the light of this we have a description of someone attempting to move beyond the limits of the physical sphere to the spiritual sphere. Of course, God cannot be tempted in this sense because he is already 'on the other side' - well, there are no sides with God, space and time need not be considered.

The word evil is *kakos* and can be translated as being of a bad nature, or being wrong. Of course God can't be wrong, he is not on one side or the other, he is inclusive of all things. This is the position we seek through our Higher Self - and the Greek word *eimi*, I am, appears in this text and is translated as the word 'for' *"for God cannot be tempted"*. Finding the right order for words in the Greek is a challenge. We could say, "(the) I Am god cannot be tempted".

James is telling us that now we each have personal responsibility for our own development when he says, *"but each person is tempted when he is lured and enticed by his own desire."* The word 'each' is *hekastos* and means each one, each individual. This again points to the post-crucifixion position of individuality, the guiding gods have withdrawn, and we are on our own. The word *'own'* is *idios* and relates to ones' self. It is the personal self; *idios* is a possessive pronoun meaning that it belongs to the person, no longer to the group.

Then we have the words, *"lured and enticed by his own desire"* which reveal the full story. Lured, *exelko,* means to draw on inward power, to lead. Enticed, *deleazo,* comes from deceived, a decoy. Lust, *epithymia,* comes from *thymos* which means anger, heat or passion.

This paints a picture of what human beings experienced at this time, and will continue to experience as we let go of the group soul and take personal responsibility for our own development. What is experienced, and what attracts our attention, is anger.

Rudolf Steiner describes anger as an educator of the soul; it achieves this by agitating the soul. The anger must be experience inwardly which strengthens us. If we express the anger we are weakened. This inner activity destroys selfishness and transforms the lower soul, the sentient soul, making it capable of love. 22.10.1909 The important thing here is that we must feel the anger. Awareness of anger assists us to use it in the right way.

Now James points out the real consequence of failing to accept full responsibility for our personal development. *"Then desire when it has conceived gives birth to sin; and sin when it is full-grown brings forth death."*

Desire, *epithymia,* refers to the underlying anger. What causes this anger? Perhaps it is the way we feel when we realize that we are totally separated from God, alone in the Universe, with a mighty task to do.

If we allow this anger to be conceived, *syllambano - lambano* means take hold of a person or thing in order to use it, we lose sight of our purpose. Then this anger gives birth, *tikto,* produces, sin. Sin is a very misunderstood word. The Greek word for sin is *hamartia* which means to miss the mark. Think of aiming an arrow and not being able to hit the bullseye. It takes practice and if we persevere we will eventually score.

Then we are told that if we do not perfect our aim it will bring forth death. 'Bring forth' is *apokyeo*; *apo*, means a separation of the part from the whole, and *kyeo* comes from *kyma* which is a wave of the sea, an impulse. Essentially we will drown in the sea of the Universe; we will lose our individuality and melt into insignificance. Then we will never become the god-beings we are destined to become.

Every experience human beings have on this earth gives us the opportunity to move forward. The choice to do so rests with each individual. This is what individuality is all about. The greatest challenge is to remain open in all circumstances so that we have the opportunity for greater understanding. Exploring the deeper meaning of Greek words reveals this. We cannot fully understand these words because we have a different consciousness, but perhaps by delving into them we can awaken past memories of a life lived 2000 years ago when we used the Greek language.

> *Do not be deceived, my beloved brethren. Every good endowment and every perfect gift is from above, coming down from the Father of lights with whom there is no variation or shadow due to change. Of his own will he brought us forth by the word of truth that we should be a kind of first fruits of his creatures. James 1:16-18*

Now James states very clearly that a new era has dawned. If we can bring to mind what it might be like to have life turned upside down, to no longer be able to live life as we did yesterday, and to find ourselves in the position of creating a completely new life, we might be able to enter into what James is saying.

The first thing to be faced is the possibility of being

misled. James points out that we receive something that has not been earned. *"every good endowment"* - endowment is *dosis* meaning gifted, freely given, and *"every perfect gift"* - perfect is *teleios* from *telos* which means that by which a thing is finished, the end to which all things relate, the aim and purpose. Gift is *dorema* meaning presented, bestowed. It came from above, *anothen*, meaning a higher place.

This gives us a sense that there was a higher purpose in this dramatic change. Nothing we could have done would change what happened. It could be compared to a catastrophic weather event. If we understand something of the evolving position of the Higher Self we find the proof of it in what James is saying. The superficial reading of the text suggests that we lowly human beings are controlled by a higher power, a Father of lights, which could be construed as God, whose will is imposed on us. Closer examination of the Greek words reveals that this higher power is *ego eimi*, the I Am.

It is important to take a close look at the next words, *"coming down from the Father of lights"*. In the Greek it says, a*nothen eimi katabaino apo pater ho phos. Anothen,* a higher place, *katabaino,* to come down, *apo* a separation of the part from the whole, *pater,* generator, *ho,* this, *phos,* light which shines or makes manifest, especially by rays.

We can express this by saying; coming down from a higher place, separating from the whole into a part, the generator, or cause of this light, shines, manifests. So, not "Father of lights", but the cause of light. This does not refer to the cause of the light in the world, but rather to the cause of the light within each person. The pronouns in this text point to the individual not a higher being like God or a broader Universe.

"With whom there is no variation or shadow due to change." This essentially means there is no longer a reflection of the Higher Self as was the case before the event of the Christen-ing of Jesus. Now the Higher Self can be experienced directly, now

human beings have the strength to bear the power of the light of this Higher Self within them. This is a significant idea, one which requires deep consideration even today. Do we take up the power of this Higher Self as we live through each day?

The word 'variation' is *parallage* meaning to change from one thing to another, a shifting. James is saying that there is no change; the Higher Self simply changes its position without changing itself. So, something that human beings could not have direct contact with because it was so powerful, they can now carry within themselves.

"*shadow due to change*" isn't quite what the Greek says. It would be better to translate these words as 'shifting shadow'. Change is really shifting, *trope,* and refers to a turning of the heavenly bodies. Shadow *aposkiasma,* from *apo*, a separation, and *skiasma* from *skia* an image cast by an object and representing the form of that object - in other words a reflection. We could take this to mean that the Higher Self is destined to be within us in its full reality, not as a reflection as it had been.

Now the full impact of this is expressed in verse 18. *"Of his own will he brought us forth by the word of truth that we should be a kind of first fruits of his creatures."* There are five different words in Greek for the noun will. This one is *boulomai* which means by deliberate design, and refers to the personal use of the will rather than having it imposed on us by an external entity.

"Brought us forth" is *apokyeo*, which means to give birth to, there is no "us", instead there is the word *ego*, which means I, me, my. "I give birth to" would be a better way of expressing this. What do I give birth to? The word of truth into this I Am or Higher Self. The Greek says *logos aletheia eis* (into), *ego eimi*, I Am.

We can forgive the translators for mistranslating these words because they did not have an understanding of the changes the Higher Self went through at the time of Christ Jesus. If we can have even a slight understanding of this we can find the truth of it in the Bible and we will be the productive first fruits.

The words 'first fruits' *aparche, is* made up of two words, *apo*, separation from the whole, and *archomai*, to be the first to do (anything), to begin. The words 'a kind of' doesn't quite express what is meant. Kind *tis*, really means a certain one, a certain thing. The last few words of this verse do not say *"of his creatures"* but rather, this themselves created. Creatures is *ktisma*, which means the product of a creative act. This last verse could read: With my own will I gave birth to the word of truth (aletheia - re-membering) into the I Am, separating it for the first time as a creative act.

Know this, my beloved brethren. Let every man be quick to hear, slow to speak, slow to anger, for the anger of man does not work the righteousness of God. Therefore put away all filthiness and rank growth of wickedness and receive with meekness the implanted word, which is able to save your souls. But be doers of the word, and not hearers only, deceiving yourselves. James 1:19-22

The first five words of this text could easily be skipped over. Some readers will receive them as a simple greeting and quickly move on to the important things James has to say. The fact is that unless these five words are understood, the rest of the text will not be fully understood. This is what they say in Greek: *Eido adelphos ego agapetos eimi.* A better translation would be: perceive the I Am brotherhood of love.

The Greek word translated as *"know this"* is *eido,* which means perceiving spiritual reality. *Adelphos* is a term meaning brotherhood, and for James this will be the brotherhood of the recently risen Christ; for when we form a conscious bond with Christ our blood changes. This is why the crucifixion was more than fixing a body to a cross; it involved the pouring out of blood from his heart into the earth.

Blood is the physical expression of our I Am and in this greeting we find the words *ego eimi*, I Am. When blood is contained it confines itself in a small group of family and race. When it is poured out it unites the whole human race. This is the focus of the brotherhood of Christ whom James now addresses. He also points out that when this true brotherhood forms, it loves in the highest way, agape.

Then James explains how we recognize those who are part of this brotherhood of love. *"Let every man be quick to hear, slow to speak, slow to anger,"*. The text does not say 'every man' but each *anthropos*, male or female, each human being, and each one individually. This means each one takes personal responsibility for themselves rather than relying on the leader of a group for guidance.

These ones are swift to hear, *akouo*, which is not just hearing but deeper hearing which comprehends spiritually. They are also slow to speak, slow to disclose their thoughts, where slow indicates giving deep consideration to the situation. They are also slow to anger, *orge*.

Understanding anger is an important part of our spiritual development as we have already explored in the word *thymos*. Thymos is the kind of anger that is more agitated and prone to outburst. *Orge* arises more slowly and is more lasting.

James continues to speak of anger and we can assume it requires extra attention. He says, *"for the anger of man does not work the righteousness of God."* The word translated as 'work' is *ergazomai* which comes from the word *ergon* meaning energy. This could be saying that human anger does not give energy to the righteousness of God. Righteousness, *dikaiosune*, means making adjustments and it is a very important word to understand.

"Righteousness, dikaiosune, means the understanding of the just, which in its truest sense is justice; the continual series of adjustments which restores balance and harmony. This refers to all the inner adjustments that we make as we develop our spiritual faculties." Who

is Jesus : What is Christ? Vol 5 by Kristina Kaine

Are human beings the only beings in the Universe to make adjustments? Surely every being in the Universe makes adjustments to restore balance according to the prevailing conditions. Therefore, can we assume that James is saying that human anger interferes with God's balancing energy?

When we experience anger do we consider that we are disturbing harmony and balance in the Universe? Furthermore, do we consider that this anger needs to be dealt with on a Universal scale by God? Would this mean that our anger distracts God from his other activities?

Then James has some quite raw things to say, *"Therefore put away all filthiness and rank growth of wickedness"* These are the Greek words James uses: therefore, *dio*, means for this reason; put away *apotithemi*. from *apo*, separate and *tithemi* to place; filthiness *rhyparia* meaning immorality, to be without conscience, without ethics, when our satisfaction is achieved at the expense of others. Rank growth is *perisseia*, meaning abundant, excessive; and wickedness is *kakia* meaning destructive. We could retranslate this by saying: For this reason separate from unethical, excessively destructive activity.

Now we come to the esoteric meaning of what James is telling us. *"and receive with meekness the implanted word, which is able to save your souls."* Meekness, *praytes*, means with gentle spirit; implanted *emphytos* is from the words, *'en'* and *'phyo'*, *en* meaning with, and *phyo*, meaning to produce.

"Which is able" does not explain what happens. The Greek is *ho* meaning that, and "able" is *dunamai* meaning power and refers to the members of the Spiritual Hierarchy called Dunamai or Powers, the spirits of movement in the Universe. They activate the word, the *logos*, not to save our souls but to keep our souls, *psyche*, safe.

"But be doers of the word, and not hearers only, deceiving

yourselves." Now James reveals the secret about the "doers". The Greek word for 'doers' is *poietes* which means author, and so "doers of the word" are logos authors. He is saying be logos authors, the word 'be' in Greek is *ginomai*, and means more than 'be', it means become, arise. The word deceiving, *paralogizomai,* means to miscount, the accounts are out of balance.

James is telling us that we now have the personal responsibility to work with God and the Spiritual Hierarchy to keep the Universe in balance. This is a mighty task.

For if any one is a hearer of the word and not a doer, he is like a man who observes his natural face in a mirror; for he observes himself and goes away and at once forgets what he was like. But he who looks into the perfect law, the law of liberty, and perseveres, being no hearer that forgets but a doer that acts, he shall be blessed in his doing. James 1:23-25

This text is quite straight forward; if we hear the truth and act on it we will be blessed. Of course, that is not all it says. If we continually remind ourselves that James is giving us advice about a new way of life after the Christ event, we can understand much more from these words.

James says, *"For if any one is a hearer of the word and not a doer, he is like a man who observes his natural face in a mirror"*. His choice of this analogy is of great consequence and contains an important esoteric secret. A *"hearer of the word"* is one who hears the Logos. James, as we have seen, places emphasis on the word, the Logos, in this chapter. The Logos is an important concept. St John begins his Gospel with the Logos; *"In the beginning was the word, the Logos"*.

In a lecture on November 10, 1904 Rudolf Steiner gives some insight into the Logos - and take note that there is more than one Logos. The Logos is integral to creation and Steiner begins this lecture by referring to the effect of the Christ event; *"We will try and get a clearer idea of the transition from the Logos to a new system, a new creation."* This is exactly what James is intent on communicating, the new creation that began when Jesus took into himself the Cosmic Christ, and the sacrifice undertaken by both these entities.

When James mentions the man observing his *"natural face in a mirror"* he reveals an important esoteric truth. Steiner continues, *"The first Logos relates to the second as if we were standing in front of our mirror image and decided to give our own life to the mirror image."* This describes sacrifice (think also of the crucifixion); the first Logos gives its life to its mirror image. The first Logos produces a reflection and then gives its life to the mirror image in sacrifice. This second Logos shines its life back onto the first Logos which is then a third Logos. If we then remind ourselves that the Logos is the word, and we think about the effect of words on those who hear it, we get a greater sense of creation caused by the word. We even experience this in our own conversation each day - some create, some destroy.

In his book "Earthly Knowledge and Heavenly Wisdom", Steiner says that the Logos is the intelligence ruling the human race that was with Father and is now with Son. February 10, 1923

Karl Konig in his book, "Becoming Aware of the Logos", speaks of the Logos in terms of the morality of creation, he says, "Morality is originary, it is the love for what does not yet exist, that it may become! Think about that in terms of the effect of our conversations, especially if we speak lovingly to people.

From these ideas we can come to a clearer understanding of our position in this world as hearers of the Logos. Hearer is *akroates* which means to understand, to perceive the sense of what is said. Then we must become doers, *poietes,* which means to make, to be authors. As we know, authors use words.

There are a few other points in this text worth noting. *"he is like a man who observes his natural face in a mirror;"* The word 'man' here is *aner* and usually refers to a male, the masculine within us. James says this man observes, *katanoeo*, *kata* means a downward motion, and *noieo*, means to consider, ponder. Then the translation says "natural face" which seems strange. Aren't all faces natural? Face is *prosopon* meaning countenance and the Greek word for 'natural' is actually *genesis* which means source or origin. The first words in the Bible are, *"In the beginning"* in the origin, the genesis. Is James saying that we can now observe our genesis countenance? Is he saying we can't move on until we see this? This would make sense if we are now to become authors, we have to see how creation occurred in the beginning which will give us clues about the way forward after the monumental event of the crucifixion and resurrection.

James continues, *"for he observes himself and goes away and at once forgets what he was like."* The words translated as 'gone away' is one word in the Greek, *aperchomai* from *apo*, meaning separation, and *erchomai*, meaning appearance. This is the man who sees his genesis countenance and then separates himself from his appearance. He is ignoring his original appearance; he wants to forget the foundation of his being, *"what he was like"*, *hopoios*, what sort of nature he had. This will not be helpful for the journey ahead.

Verse 25 says, *"But he who looks into the perfect law, the law of liberty, and perseveres, being no hearer that forgets but a doer that acts, he shall be blessed in his doing."*

There are 17 Greek words for 'look'. This one is *parakypto* from *para* aside, and *kypto*, to bend forward, telling us to stoop down and look into the perfect law. Perfect is *teleios*, and law, *nomos*, which refers to a thing that is finished, accomplished and brings liberty - *eleutheria* freedom, unrestrained, no longer a slave. James is suggesting that this can only be achieved by having the courage to look at the full spectrum of human evolution.

If any one thinks he is religious, and does not bridle his tongue but deceives his heart, this man's religion is vain. Religion that is pure and undefiled before God and the Father is this: to visit orphans and widows in their affliction, and to keep oneself unstained from the world. James 1:26-27

James now hits home by comparing the religious expression of his time with his own experience of the presence of the resurrected Christ. This is a challenge that we still face today. As we begin to experience the esoteric or underlying truth, we can then struggle to live in the culture of our time. The values of those around us can be quite different to the values emerging in us as we learn to see through the eyes of the risen Christ.

Our task is to create our own relationship with Christ through an understanding that he fully penetrated the body and blood of Jesus and experienced death. In this way he was the first spiritual being in the Universe to experience death. Through his death his blood poured into the earth changing it forever. Everything on this earth; minerals, plants and animals, contains the presence of Christ. Our task is to understand this new relationship and make it part of our everyday life.

The first thing that happens is that we become more prayerful, we genuinely value everything and everyone we encounter. James says, *"If any one thinks he is religious"* where the word 'thinks' *dokeo*, means to form an opinion which is either right or wrong, they are on the wrong track. Opinions are formed from a lack of understanding. Since the Christ event everyone has the ability to understand how this event changed the world.

The world, *kosmos*, or Universe, means that which is ordered, arranged in a particular way. The Christ event didn't just change this earth it reordered the whole Universe. Christ no longer dwells only in the higher regions of the Universe; he has penetrated this earth which has become his body. The etheric and astral forces of this earth are also penetrated by him. Our task is to form ideas about what this means for our own life. This earth has become a spiritual sun, shining out into the Universe. We can begin by creating images of this. As each person experiences the presence of Christ in this earth and in their own life, this spiritual sun shines brighter. James is telling us that any other religious expression is empty.

The Greek word for religion is *threskeia* and refers to an external religious expression with its ceremonies and practices. These can be empty expressions of worship leading us to fear God. This kind of religion was part of the dying consciousness at the time of Christ. It was used to frighten people into worshipping what the religious leaders thought (*dokeo*) was the right thing to do. The word for religion comes from *throeo* which means to cry aloud, which is why James says that we should bridle our tongue. This shows a lack of understanding and this religion is in vain. Vain *mataios* means empty.

Empty religion will no longer serve any purpose. In fact, this empty religion will hide the presence of Christ from us. Unless we can bring the living presence of Christ into our lives we continue to live in the past.

Then James says something strange, *"Religion that is pure and undefiled before God and the Father is this: to visit orphans and widows in their affliction, and to keep oneself unstained from the world."*

It is possible that the word 'religion' does not appear in the original Greek? It doesn't seem to fit with this verse because the word 'religion' is the same word *threskos* meaning fearing God, to tremble, be frightened. That is part of the past. We must now be pure and undefiled. Pure is *katharos* and means being cleansed, purified - of the influence of opinions. Undefiled *amiantos* means to dye another color.

Then we can ask why on earth we would need *"to visit orphans and widows in their affliction"*? Orphans are those deprived of parents, teachers, or guardians. So they are alone, they are the ones who experience their individuality. Widows, *chera*, also points to being alone, being stripped bare. *"In their affliction" thlipsis,* means pressure, the kind of pressure involved in pressing grapes. This pressure reshapes the orphans and widows.

This would describe what happens in our soul as the presence of Christ interrupts the normal flow of life. The parents and teachers in our soul who have been responsible for our habitual thinking are removed. The widows in our soul are stripped bare of the semi-conscious feelings which direct automatic responses to life.

During all of this activity within us as we awaken the inner presence of Christ, we have *"to keep oneself unstained from the world."* Keep *tereo,* means to attend to carefully; and unstained, *aspilos,* means free from censure, criticism. This is important advice because we have to look after ourselves as we go through the changes that the presence of Christ brings to our soul. We will only remain unstained if we refrain from preaching to others and focus on being an example of the change that comes about from the presence of Christ within and around us.

CHAPTER 2
JAMES 2

My brethren, show no partiality as you hold the faith of our Lord Jesus Christ, the Lord of glory. For if a man with gold rings and in fine clothing comes into your assembly, and a poor man in shabby clothing also comes in, and you pay attention to the one who wears the fine clothing and say, "Have a seat here, please," while you say to the poor man, "Stand there," or, "Sit at my feet," have you not made distinctions among yourselves, and become judges with evil thoughts? James 2:1-4

We have reached a point in our evolution where it is very important to see the spirit in every human being as well as to find the spirit in ourselves. We can only do this if we learn to distinguish between our physical expression, our soul expression, and our spiritual expression. Unless we do this we will not be able to make the kinds of decisions that create the future. Perhaps we can begin by deepening our understanding of the ways in which we do, in fact, create the future.

James begins by saying, *"show no partiality"*. The word 'partiality' gives us a clue. In Greek it is *prosopolepsia* which means respect or acceptance of others. Surely he is not saying show no respect for others. *Prosopolepsia* comes from two Greek words, *prosopon* meaning countenance or appearance, and *lambano*, meaning to take in order to use, to take upon oneself. This is saying that we should take in what we see, avoiding a superficial glance. When we take in what we see, that image lives in us, it becomes a living imagination which we can experience in all its reality.

The order of the Greek words is not always straightforward which makes Bible interpretation challenging. Only if we work with the words can new understanding arise. One clue comes from the use of the word 'glory' *doxa*. The words *"Lord of glory"* are not in the text. The glory of the Lord Jesus Christ is a better translation. Glory, *doxa*, means glorified, shining like a star. The star within us is our astral and when we can override its instinctual behavior our light shines. This happens when we purify our soul of its bias and allow ourselves to bring to life the inner experience of what we see.

Then James speaks about the way bias arrives in our soul - the ways in which we feel, think and act. He speaks of when the rich man and the poor man "comes into your assembly". Comes, *eiserchomai*, means come into being. This is a way to describe thoughts and feelings arising in our soul, it is also a way of describing how things come to life in our spirit, in our spiritual Imagination. As we have feeling, thinking and willing in our soul, we have Imagination, Inspiration, and Intuition in our spirit.

The word assembly is *synagoge* from *synago* which means to gather, or to lead, or direct. We can also apply this to our soul, the place where our consciousness gathers, the place where we lead and direct with our will. Equally it can point to the gathering of living or pure thinking, feeling and will in our spirit.

James describes two types of images, one with fine clothes; fine is *lampros*, shining like a lamp, and the other poor, *ptochos*, meaning crouching, fearful, lacking (it doesn't say man in the Greek). The shine from a lamp is artificial compared with the shine from a star, the *doxa*. This is our challenge, how do we discern the true value of all that meets us in our soul. The only way is with the assistance of our spirit. If we rely on the values of the physical world we will misjudge many things. In fact, we will *"become judges with evil thoughts"*. The Greek word translated as evil is *poneros*, which means worthless, of no value.

This is our task, to find value. Many of the values in society are misinformed and misleading. We have to continually make distinctions, *diakrino,* which means to separate all the elements before making decisions. Is our attention drawn to the shiny things and do we look away from *ptochos*? *Ptochos* comes from the word *ptoeo* which means to be terrified. It also speaks of descending from a higher place to a lower place. While this gives us a sense of falling and the fear that entails, it also describes incarnating into the physical world.

Are we in this poor state shabbily clothed? Shabby is *rhyparos* meaning dirty, defiled. Are we living our lives in fear, attracted to shiny things? We need courage, courage found in the glory of the Lord Jesus Christ, to separate all the elements before us and come to the right decisions. This is not a call to religious worship; this is a call to identify the Lord, the *kurios* within us. The Lord of our being is our I Am, our Higher Self.

Every single human being has a Higher Self regardless of appearance. If, when we look at any human being, we recognize this truth, we create *doxa*, glory, in the Universe. We see each human being as a being of body, soul, and spirit, not just a body clothed in shiny or dirty things. When we do this we transform the person in front of us, they are no longer defined by their outer appearance, they are seen for who they truly are.

Listen, my beloved brethren. Has not God chosen those who are poor in the world to be rich in faith and heirs of the kingdom which he has promised to those who love him? But you have dishonored the poor man. Is it not the rich who oppress you, is it not they who drag you into court? Is it not they who blaspheme that honorable name which was invoked over you? If you really fulfil the royal law, according to the scripture, "You shall love your neighbor as yourself," you do well. But if you show partiality, you commit sin, and are convicted by the law as transgressors. James 2:5-9

James now speaks intensely about love by saying, "Listen, my beloved". Beloved is *agapetos*, the highest love human beings can experience. The Greeks had many words for love which accurately described the kind of love being expressed. *Eros*, physical love; *philia*, love of brothers, sisters, friends; *storge*, love of family, tribe or nation; and *agapao*, spiritual love beyond barriers. We experience *agapao* love when we are able to unite with the true purpose of the Mystery of Golgotha. Jesus could only have participated in this mystery by experiencing the fullness of *agapao*. Therefore the presence of Christ in this world depended on *agapao*.

This is the love expressed by those who experience the highest in themselves; they express it without fear or favor. It speaks of unification and intense compassion. It may not always be interpreted as love because in its expression it can cut like a sword.

Our task is to love with this highest love, completely free of any egotistical tendencies. When we are able to experience this love we have no thought of benefits for ourselves, directly or indirectly. This love is actually the substance of the I Am and when we are able to express it we show that our I Am is active in this world.

James continues with the metaphors of rich and poor because they give the best picture of earthly judgment. The rich or wealthy, *plousios,* abound in external possessions. We only see them externally; we don't look into their souls.

Those who consider themselves rich dishonor, *atimazo,* deem unworthy, the poor. The poor may not actually be poor, but they do not place value on external possessions. They experience the highest love for others, as well as for themselves. When we experience the truth about Golgotha, when we see the deed carried out by Jesus and Christ, we immediately experience *agapao*, we become *"those who love him."* The 'him' *autos* can be God and it can also be him, her, himself, herself. In fact the statement doesn't need 'him', it could just say "those who love". This love cannot be confined by anything. Once it is experienced it cannot be contained. It is felt by all those around us and everywhere in the cosmos.

Georg Kuhlewind in his book, "Becoming Aware of the Logos", speaks about love as requiring continual effort because when we incarnate on this earth in a physical body we feel separated from others. *"Human love has to bridge a separation. It has to arise continuously anew out of the transformation of self-love. Because it is living it has no past."* We meet these ideas in the words of James.

James is trying to explain that our love in wrongly motivated most of the time. We don't transform our self-love. We love others when we can benefit from them and discard them when they are no longer useful. Whenever we are with people in our community we can apply this principal to reach an understanding of how it works. Whenever we recognize that we are drawn to someone for our benefit we awaken our soul a bit more. We only reach the highest love when we, through self-awareness, harmonize thinking, feeling, and willing in our soul. Then we can overcome our bias and love beyond earthly limits.

The rich are never happy when the 'poor' express the highest love. *"Is it not they* (the rich) *who blaspheme that honorable name which was invoked over you?"* The word 'honorable' is *basilikos*, meaning belonging to a king, royal. When *agapao* love is awakened in our souls we have regal qualities. We rule within our soul, we control our thinking, feeling and willing, harmonizing them. This is required if our I Am is to come to expression, which in turn awakens the presence of Christ. A close study of all the elements of the crucifixion and resurrection reveals all the stages of this process which every human being on the earth must experience.

This is the royal, *basilikos*, law, which we are called to fulfil. *"You shall love your neighbor as yourself,"* which does not start with the neighbor but with ourselves. Each day we should assess our love for ourselves. This love is not only for all that is good about us, it is also applies to our flaws. Can we love our flaws by recognizing that they are in the process of becoming perfected? The Greek word for sin speaks of this. Sin is *hamartia* and means to miss the mark. We can see the archer pulling on the bow string, aiming the arrow at the bullseye but not quite hitting the mark. Surely we can love the archer for his diligence. In this way we can also love ourselves. Out to this love for ourselves we can love others, including all those who miss the mark.

For whoever keeps the whole law but fails in one point has become guilty of all of it. For he who said, "Do not commit adultery," said also, "Do not kill." If you do not commit adultery but do kill, you have become a transgressor of the law. So speak and so act as those who

are to be judged under the law of liberty. For judgment is without mercy to one who has shown no mercy; yet mercy triumphs over judgment. James 2:10-13

This text states the situation as it is. The law is now the royal law of love. If we love then we will naturally keep all the commandments mentioned in the Old Testament. Law, *nomos,* comes from a primary Greek word *nemo* which means to parcel out, especially food or grazing to animals. We get a sense of allocation and also a sense of survival if the right allocation is made. Laws are not an imposition they are guidelines for survival.

Since the resurrection of Christ we have moved from the Ten Commandments to the One Commandment. *"A new commandment I give to you, that you love one another; even as I have loved you, that you also love one another."* John 13:34 We should consider these words daily and apply them with every encounter throughout the day, as well as to our private thoughts about others.

Keeping the whole law, *tereo,* meaning to attend to it carefully, to take care of it, and this becomes our only task. We no longer need to go through all ten laws if we love. The examples James gives here about adultery and killing are worth considering. He will have chosen them purposefully. There is only one Greek word for adultery *moicheuo* and it means to be faithless or unfaithful. We slip into faithlessness when we lose sight of the reality of Christ which is so easy to do at this time when we are grappling to understand who this Mighty Being really is. We can stumble, fall to a lower place, into emotional and sentimental ideas about God, and turn our back on Christ with whom we vowed to create a relationship.

The word for kill here is *phoneuo* which means destroy. If we are guilty, *enochos,* meaning that we are entangled, of this destruction what are we doing? Essentially it means that we destroy the presence of Christ in others. We could ask ourselves if we judge Christ as we read about him in the New Testament. If we say no, then why do we judge others who have Christ within them? They may be 'missing the mark' but that doesn't mean they do not have Christ within them. If we kill Christ within them through our attitude to them they will certainly have a greater struggle to find him. Then we become transgressors, *parabates,* meaning to go past or pass over without touching.

All the aspects of the Mystery of Golgotha should occupy our thoughts often. Not that we should continually grapple with an intellectual understanding of what took place. We certainly should not form judgments of what took place. This Deed will only reveal itself fully in the future. In the meantime we can hold the idea of the Deed in our minds as a meditation, however short. Then drop it and carry on with our day. The power of the Deed will grow within us over time, and over lifetimes.

Then James focuses on judgment. He says that we should now speak and act under the law of liberty, *eleutheria,* freedom, which means not to live as we please but to live as we should. This involves mercy, *eleos,* which means goodwill and compassion. This is the kind of will we must now use; our own will, not the will of some guiding power.

We can recognize many elements of the Mystery of Golgotha here. When the resurrected Christ is absorbed into the region of our soul called the Intellectual Soul, the 'I' manifests more. Then judgment looks to future possibilities not just present expressions and this leads to mercy, to goodwill, to kindness. The Intellectual Soul then becomes a soul of mercy.

Judgment is that higher ability not be swayed by our self-will, or the will of others. Judgment in Greek is *krisis,* a process of assessment and means separating (analyzing) before a decision is made. Yet how often do we separate out all the facts?

We have the ability for accurate assessment when our I-being emerges as an independent entity in our soul. Then we truly love because love is reborn in the 'I', it reaches a higher expression, *agapao*. This is the true meaning of liberty, of freedom.

Taking all these elements into consideration we can see how *"mercy triumphs over judgment"*. The word triumph, *katakauchaomai*, means towards glory, and when we experience glory the presence of Christ shines in our soul. Christ is crucified in our lower expressions and raises us, resurrects in us, so that we shine out his presence. We don't need to explain this, people get it. They are touched because it resonates with the presence of Christ within them. When this resonance takes place the resurrection process is enlivened with them as well. This transforms their judging and their mercy and the highest love becomes more active within all of us.

What does it profit, my brethren, if a man says he has faith but has not works? Can his faith save him? If a brother or sister is ill-clad and in lack of daily food, and one of you says to them, "Go in peace, be warmed and filled," without giving them the things needed for the body, what does it profit? So faith by itself, if it has no works, is dead. But some one will say, "You have faith and I have works." Show me your faith apart from your works, and I by my works will show you my faith. You believe that God is one; you do well. Even the demons believe--and shudder. James 2:14-19

If we are observant we find within human beings the deep need to profit. We could say that it is part of our survival mechanism. Profit, *ophelos*, means to heap up, to accumulate. If we examine our own lives we find this impulse in many aspects of our lives, not only with possessions but also with thoughts, feelings, and actions. Then we discover how selfish and self-centered it is to want to accumulate more than other people.

Is this instinct to accumulate grounded in our deep, subconscious sense of loss? James uses the example of the ill-clad brother or sister. Ill-clad, *gymnos,* means without clothing, naked. We met this idea at the beginning of the Bible in the story of Adam and Eve. *"And the man and his wife were both naked and were not ashamed."* Genesis 2:25

In the translation of the words of James, one word is not translated which is *hyparcho*. In Greek, the order of the words can be fluid and so it is difficult to know where this missing word really belongs. The Greek text reads *gymnos hyparcho; hypo*, means under, and *archo* is from *archomai*, which means to be the first to do anything. This points back to Genesis where Adam and Eve were the first to be naked.

Food, *trophe,* means nourishment rather than food substance. On this earth we are naked and lack daily nourishment for our spiritual sustenance. In this condition we find two kinds of people; those who reject faith, and those who have blind faith. Both perspectives show a lack of understanding for the true human being.

Faith, *pistis,* is a very important word to comprehend. Until we comprehend it we cannot have faith. Faith needs works, *ergon,* energy. Faith is actually a clairvoyant power which sees behind the physical, it is a foreseeing knowledge not a substitute for knowledge.

Rudolf Steiner made this important statement about faith. *"Faith is the capacity of going beyond oneself, of flowing out beyond that which I can do for my own self perfection. Receiving Christ into our I."* Cycle of the Year p123

Rev Mario Schoenmaker said, *"Faith – pistis – is not believing ideas but the grasping of a growing reality in the supersensible world, and making it the concern of one's own will. Seeing a possibility, making the outcome our own concern, which develops a spiritual force which doesn't bear witness but determines the outcome. One learned about him, and got to know him."* 19.8.1994

Faith therefore is a cognitive experience not a substitute for cognition. So faith without works, energy, is dead, *nekros*, lifeless. James asks, *"Can his faith save him?"* The word for 'can' is *dunamai*, which means power and directs our attention to the Spiritual Hierarchy, way above the Angels and Archangels. Before we incarnated into this earth we dwelt with this ninefold Hierarchy, and when we first came to this earth, as the story of Adam and Eve describes, we were led by this Hierarchy until we found our own feet.

We might ask why James is placing so much emphasis on the body in this text. We are threefold beings of body, soul and spirit. Body, s*oma,* differentiates from our soul which is *psuche,* and our spirit which is *pneuma.* Our soul and spirit need this body so that through our own efforts we can be reborn, resurrected, into our true spiritual beingness.

James is pointing out the importance of looking after the body - not just physically but also spiritually, so that we can fulfil our purpose on this earth. The one who says, *"Go in peace, be warmed and filled,"* has no regard for the importance of the body without which human beings cannot have the power of faith, and work with the Powers of the Hierarchy. These Powers are also known as Dunamai, they are the spirits of movement, and they brought the cosmos into movement. It is interesting that the Greek word for 'can' is *dunamai* because it does speak of power. In other places in the Bible it is also translated as able.

Then James says, *"You believe that God is one;"* Believe *pisteuo,* is from the word faith and means to think to be true, and suggests a lack of confidence. Often when people speak of God there is a lack of confidence, of not knowing who or what this being really is.

The word for 'one' is *eimi,* meaning am, which is part of

the statement *ego eimi*, I Am. When we speak of a Hierarchy of beings higher than ourselves, Angels, Archangels, Dunamai, etc., above all these is God. Often when people speak of God they don't reach any higher than their experience of their Guardian Angel. We could also say that our God is our I Am, that higher being to which we aspire. God is certainly the source of the human I Am.

"You do well" is an understatement. Do is *poieo* and means to make, produce, to be the author; well, *kalos*, really means beautiful, excellent. James is saying that if we can see the stature of the I Am we make ourselves beautiful. This beauty shines from us as evidence of our success. This causes the demons to shudder, to tremble with fear, because it signals their demise.

Do you want to be shown, you shallow man, that faith apart from works is barren? Was not Abraham our father justified by works, when he offered his son Isaac upon the altar? You see that faith was active along with his works, and faith was completed by works, and the scripture was fulfilled which says, "Abraham believed God, and it was reckoned to him as righteousness"; and he was called the friend of God. You see that a man is justified by works and not by faith alone. And in the same way was not also Rahab the harlot justified by works when she received the messengers and sent them out another way? For as the body apart from the spirit is dead, so faith apart from works is dead. James 2:20-26

James continues to emphasize the importance of faith backed up by energetic works. Our choice is to skip over this repetition or to take it seriously and look more deeply into it.

A different translation of the first verse gives a slightly different view: Will you know deeply O empty human beings that faith separate from works is free of labor. The word translated as "want" *thelo,* is will, the soul function we are currently working on. We mostly use it unconsciously at present but our task is to become increasingly aware of its activity within us. "Shown" is *ginosko,* which means 'to know deeply' and is a Jewish idiom for sexual intercourse. "Shallow" *kenos,* means empty, and man is *anthropos* - human beings of either gender. "Faith" *pistis,* means insightful knowledge not a substitute for knowledge. "Apart" *choris,* means separate, from "works", *ergon,* meaning energy, is barren *argo*s, meaning free of labor.

There is great purpose behind using Abraham as an example, not simply because Abraham did what God told him and prepared to sacrifice his only son. Abraham is an important pillar in the history of the human race. The Matthew Jesus descended from Abraham.

"The book of the genealogy of Jesus Christ, the son of David, the son of Abraham. Abraham was the father of Isaac, and Isaac the father of Jacob, and Jacob the father of Judah and his brothers," Mt 1:1-2

In his lecture on the Gospel of St Matthew, Lecture 5, Rudolf Steiner speaks about the role of the blood in this lineage which facilitates the birth of one of the two Jesus', the Matthew Jesus.

"In the composition of this blood - which was needed by the Zarathustra-Individuality for the fulfillment of his great mission - there was inner order and harmony, reflecting one of the most beautiful and significant principles manifest in the heavenly constellations. The blood available for Zarathustra was therefore an image of the Cosmos, having been prepared through generations in accordance with cosmic law."

I explain a lot about Abraham in my series Who is Jesus : What is Christ? Here is one aspect.

Abraham's faith was so strong that he was even prepared to sacrifice his only legitimate son Isaac; an act which echoes God sacrificing his son Christ and so, no doubt, Abraham was already preparing for the mystery of Golgotha. His faith made Abraham the father of the Hebrew race out of which Jesus could be born who became the bearer of Christ. Who is Jesus : What is Christ? Volume 1

If we pause to think about this it becomes clear that the evolution of the human race was planned over eons. It reveals that is not just the contribution of our past lives but also our physical ancestry that makes us who we are. We also incarnate through the ages to experience the different stages of evolution and in this way contribute to the character of the future. If we live our lives with this understanding we work as co-creators with the mighty beings who lead the way. This is the real point James makes; today, in every moment of our lives, we create the future. This requires energetic work on our part; faith won't do it. This energetic work involves understanding evolution and our place in it. The Bible is a very important tool for this work, the true meaning of its words has been preserved esoterically. We are called to energetically bring this true meaning to light within ourselves.

Then, somewhat surprisingly, James uses the example of a harlot. Here is a simple explanation of Rahab: Rahab was a harlot in Jericho who helped the messengers escape, saving the destruction of Jericho; married Salmon, an ancestor of David and of Christ; and is commended for her faith by James.

To make sense of Rahab's activity it helps to understand the nature of the harlot who sells sex rather than gives it away. In my interpretation of the harlot in the book of Revelation I said, "The harlot is not the subject of moral judgment; she is the one who does what she likes regardless of the spiritual principles she knows. There is a sense that she is too lazy to continue with her spiritual development. She had a taste of it, some successes, and that was enough." Kristina Kaine, The Virgin and The Harlot

To further understand what James is saying we should ask: Who were the messengers that Rahab received and sent out another way? The word messenger is *angelos*, Angels. The word for receive is *dechomai* which can mean to receive or grant access to, not to refuse intercourse or friendship. Did Rahab have intercourse with Angels? Was it sexual or was it simply a deeply intimate exchange where she was able to assist the Angels to understand what was taking place in evolution? This would be the work of the body intimately connected to the spirit. As James says, *"For as the body apart from the spirit is dead, so faith apart from works is dead."* The body apart from the spirit is the harlot.

CHAPTER 3
JAMES 3

Let not many of you become teachers, my brethren, for you know that we who teach shall be judged with greater strictness. For we all make many mistakes, and if any one makes no mistakes in what he says he is a perfect man, able to bridle the whole body also. If we put bits into the mouths of horses that they may obey us, we guide their whole bodies. Look at the ships also; though they are so great and are driven by strong winds, they are guided by a very small rudder wherever the will of the pilot directs. James 3:1-4

When the esoteric aspect of the Bible begins to reveal itself to us we have the impulse to share it. This is partly because of the joy we feel as we see the new meaning of the words, but it is also because we want to guide people away from false ideas. The way the first verse is translated is typical of a teacher who thinks they know better than most. These are the ones who say; don't do this because that will happen to you.

Since the crucifixion and resurrection of Christ, now that his presence is with us, in and around this earth, we no longer need teachers. All we need is to understand the basic principles of life on this earth, especially the fact that we are here to unfold the power of our I Am, and as we do truth will be revealed to us. This will not happen through an external teacher but through inner revelations. These revelations will be the reward for our effort. Then we become a living example of truth.

Perhaps a better way to express the first verse will give us a greater understanding of what James is saying: Not many teachers come into existence discerning, my brother, because greater judgment is needed in order to use it.

What does it mean to need greater judgment in order to be a teacher? For the most part it means keeping our mouths shut. James is not giving advice to those who don't know and try to teach, but to those who do know so that they refrain from teaching. He goes on to speak about this by using the metaphor of a horse's mouth and a bridle. If we place these ideas into our daily life when we are with family and friends who say things we know are not true, James is saying that we should restrain our response. Even if we are asked for our opinion we should restrain ourselves from pointing out the errors. The fact that someone has asked the question tells us that their inner teacher is at work. As they grapple with the issue, the truth of it will be revealed within them.

We are in a stage of human evolution where each person must make the effort themselves to come to truth. James says, *"if any one makes no mistakes in what he says he is a perfect man,"* We get a sense that by paying attention to our own development we walk with others who are doing the same. The word 'mistake' is really offend, *ptaio*, which means to cause one to stumble, to fall down. We know this is what happens when we give people advice. Their reaction distracts them from their higher path of self-discovery.

James is saying that by restraining our response in any situation we leave a space, a stoma - translated here as "mouth". Making "no mistakes in what he says" is a very misleading translation of the Greek. The word 'says' is *logos,* the creative word. A better translation is that if we do not cause anyone to stumble (by giving them unwanted advice) we are the perfect human being. The word perfect is also misleading, *teleios,* really means mature, complete. James is saying that we will be in touch with our true human potential. This potential means that we are "able to bridle," the word 'able' is *dynatos*, meaning powerful, strong, from *dunamai*, the fifth level in the spiritual Hierarchy, the spirits of movement who brought the cosmos into movement.

Bridle is an interesting word. *Chalinagogeo* means to lead, hold in check and comes from two words, *chalinos*, a bridle, and *ago*, which means to lead, to take with one, to lead by accompanying. So it is not by controlling but by accompanying that we come to perfection together. This gives us the sense of working in community with others. This is the new community we are creating, not by instructing others, but by being the person who can contribute to this community through personal development.

The word 'body' needs to be understood if we are to make sense of what James is saying. This quote will explain it more clearly.

"Our body, *soma,* includes our etheric and lower astral - all that is physically required to sustain life on this earth. *Soma* differentiates our body from our soul which is *psuche* and our spirit which is *pneuma*. Our soul and spirit need this body so that through our own efforts we can be reborn, resurrected, into our true spiritual beingness. We cannot do this in the spiritual worlds, we can only do it on this earth." Kristina Kaine Who is Jesus : What is Christ? Vol 5

The metaphor of bits and rudders says it all. These very small items have a great impact. The word 'bits' is *chalinos* which comes from the word bridle, *chalao*, which means to loosen, relax, let down from a higher place to a lower. This reinforces the sense that the smallest response has the greatest impact.

So the tongue is a little member and boasts of great things. How great a forest is set ablaze by a small fire! And the tongue is a fire. The tongue is an unrighteous world among our members, staining the whole body, setting on fire the cycle of nature, and set on fire by hell. For every kind of beast and bird, of reptile and sea creature, can be tamed and has been tamed by humankind, but no human being can tame the tongue--a restless evil, full of deadly poison. With it we bless the Lord and Father, and with it we curse men, who are made in the likeness of God. From the same mouth come blessing and cursing. My brethren, this ought not to be so. James 3:5-10

Now James lets loose on human nature. He is using his own 'tongue' to point out the responsibility of every human being to become conscious of the way they use their tongue. He is not just referring to the physical use of the tongue but also the inner forming of ideas that can be expressed using the tongue. Is our tongue guided by our self-centered ego (associated with our astral) or by our I Am?

To fully understand the importance of these ideas we should place the development of the tongue front and center. Every child develops the capacity to form speech through the use of their tongue after they learn to walk. It is part of the process of acquiring the human I-being. It is this I-being that sets us apart from animals. We can call it our individuality, our ability to self-determine, and it is also connected to our ability to become God-beings. We were gifted the potential of this I-being when Adam and Eve left the spiritual words taking on physical bodies to enable them to live on the earth as independent beings. We were gifted personal use of this I-being when Christ entered the body of Jesus on the cross on Golgotha.

Rudolf Steiner spoke often about the three stages of development of the child pointing out that this is what makes us the most highly developed beings on the earth. The three capacities that set us apart are walking, speaking, and thinking.

"Learning to speak is the second capacity which a child acquires before the actual Ego-consciousness [I-consciousness] awakens, the awakening coming after he has learnt to speak. Learning to speak depends altogether on a kind of imitation, the aptitude for which, however, is deeply embedded in human nature. Speech came to man as a consequence of progressive development. The Spirits of Form [Elohim or Exousiai] poured themselves into man and permeated him, and thereby he became able to speak a language, to live his earth life on the physical plane. [...] through the upright position and speech, he wrests himself free from those spiritual forces that are active upon the Earth. Animals are permeated by those forces; they do not in reality speak." Pre-Earthly Deeds of Christ Rudolf Steiner, March 7, 1914

James directs our attention to the animal kingdom in verse 7 although the words can be a bit misleading. *"For every kind of beast and bird, of reptile and sea creature, can be tamed and has been tamed by humankind."* James is speaking about these animal natures within us which we can express using our tongue.

This helps us understand why James uses the tongue to awaken us to the human potential within each of us when he says the tongue is *"a restless evil, full of deadly poison."* Taming the tongue is about restraining it, *amazo*. Restless is *akatastatos* which also means unstable. Evil, *kakos, means* destructive, and *"full of deadly poison"*, *thanatephoros*, means death-bringing.

Broadly speaking we could say that evolution depends on

the use of the tongue. Each human being has the opportunity, and responsibility, to advance human evolution and the evolution of the entire cosmos, through the way they use their tongue. James is saying that restraining the unstable tongue also restrains all that is destructive and will therefore be life-giving.

Then, in verse 9 James says man is made in the likeness of God. In the Greek it says *homoiosis theos ginomai* which really means 'making like God to become' or by changing the order of the words, as we can with the Greek language, 'making to become like God' - this is James reminding us that we are destined to become gods. Psalm 82 states this very clearly *"I say, 'You are gods, sons of the Most High, all of you;'"* Psalm 82:6

What James is really telling us in these verses is that human freedom is centered on the use of the tongue. Through the use of our tongue we have the choice to create or destroy. This already speaks to us of a god-like capacity. Do we think of this every time we speak, think, or write words? (Not forgetting that the word is the Logos.) We can associate this with the principles of reproduction and think of our lips as female, our tongue as male, and our words are the child we produce.

This child has a life of its own, as does every child born into this world. Our task is to give this child the best opportunity to be creative in the world. We can assist the process by becoming much more aware of what lies behind each word we speak - each child we create. If we consciously control the forming of words through our speech and thinking, which we can say is 'minding our tongue'; we develop a greater feeling for the truth, and the purpose of our tongue is to seek to produce truth - to give blessing, *eulogia*. Then we give ourselves time to weigh up the importance of our words and to think of the consequences that arise from the words we speak.

Does a spring pour forth from the same opening fresh water and brackish? Can a fig tree, my brethren, yield olives, or a grapevine figs? No more can salt water yield fresh. Who is wise and understanding among you? By his good life let him show his works in the meekness of wisdom. But if you have bitter jealousy and selfish ambition in your hearts, do not boast and be false to the truth. This wisdom is not such as comes down from above, but is earthly, unspiritual, devilish. For where jealousy and selfish ambition exist, there will be disorder and every vile practice. But the wisdom from above is first pure, then peaceable, gentle, open to reason, full of mercy and good fruits, without uncertainty or insincerity. And the harvest of righteousness is sown in peace by those who make peace. James 3:11-18

The first verse is a good example of the ways in which translators reveal their inability to understand what is being said in these ancient Greek words. Firstly, the word 'water' is not in the original, nor the words 'fresh' and 'brackish' - the Greek words are sweet and bitter. The word 'spring' *pege*, means fountain or spring and comes from *pegnymi* which means to make fast, to build by fastening together. We could take it to mean spring into existence. Opening, *ope*, means an aperture through which one can see, and comes from *optanomai*, meaning to look at, behold, or to allow one's self to be seen.

Through the word 'spring' is James asking us if we are building ourselves up by fastening ourselves together, in other words, connecting together all our bodies; physical, etheric, astral and I, so that we can pour outwardly from ourselves instead of focusing inwardly. We create an opening through which we can see but also we allow ourselves to be seen in both our sweetness *glykys* and bitterness *pikros*.

This is such an important message for us to contemplate.

How often do we present ourselves as a fig tree when we are really producing olives? It could be helpful for us to observe who we think we are when we are with various people. Even though we present ourselves in a certain way, can the other person see through that to who we really are? When will we reach the stage in our development feeling confident to be open and honest with each other? We can only reach this stage when we truly love, when we experience the highest form of love, *agape*, for ourselves as well as for others.

Then James asks: *"Who is wise and understanding among you?"* Wise is *sophos*, and knowledgeable *epistemon*, which means to put one's attention on, fix one's thoughts on. This, he says, is the "good life", *anastrophe*, which really means our conduct, and comes from the word *anastrepho* which means to turn one's self about or to turn back. This points to the idea of being true to ourselves, not inventing a persona.

James says that this also requires *"meekness of wisdom"*. Meekness is *praytes*, meaning mildness of disposition, gentleness of spirit. Wisdom is *sophia* which is also the name of the mother of Jesus the Christ-ened one.

We can see that the message is to experience this earth fully; it offers us the opportunity to become conscious of the spiritual worlds through our own effort while we live on this earth. The life we experience in this physical world does not come from the physical world; it comes from the spiritual world. We cannot understand this life through physical laws; we have to find the spiritual life that is within, and sustains, everything physical. Isn't this what the word *anastrepho* is telling us? We must turn ourselves around to see the spirit that sustains every physical thing, including every person.

When we have this view we will be wise and understanding, and we will be gentle in our dealings with others. We are quick to think we can be honest with others, but if our honesty causes a reaction we have acted too soon. To be wise and understanding means we have developed our connection with our Higher Self to the point that we are able to stand in their shoes, to experience their position from their point of view, and to respond in a gentle and understanding way. Just as we often do not know what other people are really thinking, we may not fully understand how we will influence them. We can be assured that we will have an effect on them if we achieve the right disposition, the gentleness of spirit. Our interactions will be filled with peace.

To achieve this peace James mentions nine principles to guide us to being open and honest with each other, which we can only achieve through our Higher Self.

The first is wisdom from above, then to be pure, *hagnos*, which means pure, sacred, and comes from *hagios* meaning most holy thing. The third is peaceable, *eirenikos*, peace is *eireno* and probably comes from a primary verb *eiro* which means to join. We can only achieve peace by responding to difficulties in a balanced way. The fourth is to be gentle, *epieikes*, meaning mild and impartial. Five is open to reason, *eupeithes*, meaning we remain open to new ideas. The sixth is full of mercy *eleos* meaning kindness, goodwill. Then seven is good fruits, *agathos karpos*, which means to have good results, good effects. Eight is without uncertainty *adiakritos*, without ambiguity, not to discriminate. The ninth is having no insincerity, *anypokritos* means undisguised.

Life will only be orderly if we live by these nine principles. Then, *"the harvest of righteousness is sown in peace by those who make peace."* Then we have the fruit (not harvest) of righteousness, where righteousness is *dikaiosune,* which means the understanding of the just, which in its truest sense is justice; the continual series of adjustments which restore balance and harmony. This refers to all the inner adjustments that we make as we develop our spiritual faculties.

CHAPTER 4
JAMES 4

What causes wars, and what causes fightings among you? Is it not your passions that are at war in your members? You desire and do not have; so you kill. And you covet and cannot obtain; so you fight and wage war. You do not have, because you do not ask. You ask and do not receive, because you ask wrongly, to spend it on your passions. Unfaithful creatures! Do you not know that friendship with the world is enmity with God? Therefore whoever wishes to be a friend of the world makes himself an enemy of God. James 4:1-4

Life on this earth depends on putting things into true perspective. If we look out into the world and see conflicts and battles we should search for their true origins. We could say that a person tries to take advantage of the person with whom they are fighting. Or one country tries to take something from another country, and so on.

James is very specific, he says, *"your passions that are at war in your members"* Passions, *hedone*, from *handano* which means to please, and refers to seeking pleasure; are at war, battling, in your members. Members, *melo*s, means parts of the human body. So this is an inner battle. The cause, the origin, must be sought within us.

While we can be inclined to apply this text to groups or countries at war with each other, when we look within us to all our inner conflicts, we can find another cause for all the conflicts on the earth. The word cause in Greek is *pothen*, and it means origin. James is saying that we need to look at the cause for the world's problems within human beings, within their members. This would suggest that if each human being could remove their inner conflicts there would be no war in the world and no fighting amongst us.

In verse one, the word 'war' appears twice. The first word for war is *polemos*, which means battle, or bustle. The second word 'war' is *strateuomai*, from *stratia*, meaning a host, a crowd. This crowd can be of soldiers or angels, or heavenly bodies. This would suggest that it is not only a personal struggle within us, a struggle that would take place in our astral and our soul, but also a struggle involving other spiritual beings around us.

This struggle arises when we desire and do not have; so we kill. Desire is lust, *epithymeo*, meaning passion - an anger flaring up and then subsiding. This desire for that which we do not possess leads us to kill, *phoneuo*, meaning murder. We can ask ourselves what we are murdering within us.

If we think about all the struggles within us as we go through life, we can connect with what James is saying here. Then, if we remind ourselves that James is explaining to us what we will experience as a result of the crucifixion and resurrection of Christ, we can perhaps take these struggles as our purpose rather than our difficulties.

Then, James says, *"we covet and cannot obtain."* Covet is *zeloo*, meaning zeal, fervor. The word cannot is *dunamai*, which introduces those beings of the Spiritual Hierarchy responsible for the movement in the Cosmos and within us. The Greek word for obtain is very interesting. It is *epitynchano*, from *epi*, meaning position, and *tynchano*, which means to hit the mark with an arrow. This directs our attention to the word 'sin' which, in the Greek, is *hamartia*, and means missing the mark. This suggests that as we try to obtain we also resist sinning.

We get a sense of the struggle we engage in without understanding the specifics of the struggle. We could even say that we are engaged in a battle and we are blindfolded. This is why the struggle is within ourselves as we strive to identify all the elements that are in conflict.

James then points out why this is. *"You ask and do not receive, because you ask wrongly, to spend it on your passions."* The Greek word for receive is *lambano*, which is not a passive receiving but rather an active taking hold of something and carrying it away with us. We ask wrongly, *kakos*, which means destructive, injurious. The word ask is *aiteo*, which has the idea of begging or craving. Then we spend it, and spend, *dapanao*, means waste. We waste what we could receive on our passions, our lusts, *hedone*.

This makes us *"unfaithful creatures" moichalis* - the translation of the Greek word *moichalis* is adulteress. This female expression of adulterer points to our feelings. These feelings place us in *"enmity with God"*. Enmity, *echthra*, comes from *echthros* which means hated. In truth, when we are unfaithful creatures we actually hate God.

What James is describing here is the battle within us when our Higher Self seeks to be expressed in our soul so that we experience the Christ Spirit within us. War breaks out. This war results from our lack of awareness about what is happening. The purpose of James' letter is to awaken us to the process of integrating the I Am and Christ within us. Once we are aware of this we can participate in the movement (*dunamai*) so that the arrow hits the bullseye.

As we become aware of this process taking place in our soul, we see how our lower soul expressions fight the change. Rather than engaging in this battle, we can observe it and make strategic decisions about the way forward.

Or do you suppose it is in vain that the scripture says, "He yearns jealously over the spirit which he has made to dwell in us"? But he gives more grace; therefore it says, "God opposes the proud, but gives grace to the humble." Submit yourselves therefore to God. Resist the devil and he will flee from you. Draw near to God and he will draw near to you. James 4:5-8

Scripture, *graphe*, means a thing written, words as we find in the Bible, which is not always popular today. Those who do read scripture often read it superficially, and those attracted to spiritual knowledge are often put off by the difficulty of understanding the hidden meaning behind the words. Scripture is never vain; it is never empty of truth. Often the simplest words contain the deepest truth. Even a simple word like 'says' which in Greek is *lego*, means to affirm, to maintain, and speaks of the need to direct our attention to deeper, inner meanings.

There is a power behind the words in the Bible, especially to the extent to which we can explore the original meaning of the Greek words. This power is energetic and if we have approached the Bible with devotion, whatever effort we invest will be enhanced. Our effort takes on energy of its own and can speak to us of things beyond our own ability to comprehend the words. As James says, we can suppose, *dokeo*, which means think and comes from *deiknyo* meaning to show, to expose to the eyes. This ability to suppose should not be superficial, it should be enhanced because it is with our inner eye that we see images, and we could take this to mean thinking-Imagination which is the first stage of spiritual understanding.

So does scripture speak to us in vain? The word vain, *kenos*, which means empty, devoid of truth, directs our attention to the importance of seeking the true meaning of the words used in scripture. What are we to make of these next words, *"He yearns jealously over the spirit which he has made to dwell in us"*? In many ways, words like this do not give us the connection to truth that creates the spiritual energy required to understand them. This whole text suggests that we give ourselves over to another power and everything will be taken care of. As we have been considering, this is far from the truth.

What is this spirit which God has made dwell in us? It is the I Am, the Higher Self. Why does he yearn jealously over this spirit? The word yearn is *epipotheo* which means to long for, to desire. Why would God long for or desire the spirit which he has made to dwell in us? Is it because he does not have this spirit, this I Am? Does this explain the use of the word jealously? In Greek, this word is *phthonos* meaning envy which comes from the word *phtheiro* which means to corrupt, to destroy. Is this what is behind the words of St John: *"Destroy this temple, and in three days I will raise it up."* John 2:19 Even the meaning of the word spirit has a sense of destruction. *Pneuma* from *pneo*, which means to breathe, to blow, of the wind.

This simple text seems to speak to us of the power of a spirit that only beings at a certain stage of the evolution of the Universe can experience in a particular way. We could take it that these beings are not gods or angels they are human beings. This spirit has been made to dwell, *katoikeo*, in us because of the crucifixion and resurrection of Christ. James is intent on helping us understand this.

As we become aware of the true nature of what has taken place we are given, *didomi*, grace. The nature of this giving is important. *Didomi* means to give freely, it is a gift, and nothing is expected in return. Expecting something in return belongs to the nature of the ego. This is something we should all examine in our lives because often our relationships are based on getting something in return.

Grace, *charis,* is what we experience in the second level of our spirit, our Life Spirit. When we begin to use this second level of spirit we experience Inspiration, the images that we created though spiritual Imagination start to breathe into us, to speak to us. Grace is also the ability to have full control over all our feelings, thoughts and actions. It is the ability to see God or the highest in everyone and everything. Then all our responses are graceful.

When we read the words, *"God opposes the proud, but gives grace to the humble"* we should become aware of the element of our ego rising up within us. When our ego rises up it is an invitation to the devil, the *diabolos*, the one prone to slander, to accusing falsely. This word comes from *diaballo* which means to throw over or across, to send over. This can mean that we throw over all that we don't like. In scripture, the word 'devil' usually refers to Lucifer. We must see him at work because we can't resist this devil if you don't identify him.

The words *"Submit yourselves therefore to God"* take away from the idea that we are working together with God. 'Submit yourselves' in the Greek is one word, *hypotasso* from *hypo*, meaning by, under, and *tasso*, to put in a certain order, to arrange. We could say that this means to put ourselves in a certain order with God, which does not mean to mindlessly think God will take care of everything. If we are integrating our I Am into our soul, and God yearns for this experience, then we will *"Draw near to God and he will draw near to you"* - God will then experience the reality of the I Am.

Cleanse your hands, you sinners, and purify your hearts, you men of double mind. Be wretched and mourn and weep. Let your laughter be turned to mourning and your joy to dejection. Humble yourselves before the Lord and he will exalt you. Do not speak evil against one another, brethren. He that speaks evil against a brother or judges his brother, speaks evil against the law and judges the law. But if you judge the law, you are not a doer of the law but a judge. There is one lawgiver and judge, he who is able to save and to destroy. But who are you that you judge your neighbor? James 4:8-12

James knows about the difficulties of navigating between earthly and spiritual life, especially the difficulty of living in both worlds at the same time. He continues to give advice about how we might do this and focusses on the soul life where we can be of double mind. What is this double mindedness? We experience it every day through sympathy and antipathy. These are critical human activities that assist us to navigate life in the physical world, and we have to be aware of them, and we have to overcome them. On one level they have their place and on another level they cause bias. In the physical world they keep our body safe, on the soul level they can prevent us from connecting with our spirit.

We are told to cleanse our hands, where cleanse is *katharizo* meaning to free ourselves from admixture. Admixture is the state of impairing the quality or reducing the value of something. If we apply this to our hands, that part of our body which expresses our will, we become aware of the power of our decisions. We can think of our hands as the means to grasp things or fold in reverence. If we don't make the right decision we miss the mark, which is what sin, *hamartia*, means.

We are also told to purify our hearts of double mind ("you men" is not in the Greek). The word purify here is *hagnizo* which comes from *hagnos*, which means reverence, sacred. If we can do this we will not be double minded. Double mind is *dipsychos* from *dis*, meaning twice and *psyche*, meaning soul. This is our sympathy and antipathy, our likes and dislikes which rise up in our soul automatically. It is in our hearts that we can direct our likes and dislikes purposefully.

Then, strangely, we are told to "be wretched" which is *talaiporeo* and comes from the base word *talanton* which means the scale of balance, that which is weighed. This confirms the activity in our soul of sympathy and antipathy being weighed and balanced. When this happens we will mourn *pentheo,* from grief, as we put aside some of life's pleasures. We will also weep, *klaio*, lament, which is a sign of pain caused by the loss of physical satisfaction.

At this point it is good to re-read the text and compare our original understanding with a more detailed understanding of the meaning of the Greek words. What seems quite negative in the text becomes more positive as we see how we can actively participate in the process.

Then we read some more strange advice. *"Let your laughter be turned to mourning and your joy to dejection."* We laugh when we do not want to understand something. We expand out of ourselves as a way of dismissing the opportunity to see the spiritual aspects. This means that we are disconnecting with our soul and spirit. The mourning process draws us into ourselves allowing us to experience the reality of our being in the physical world without any experience of the spiritual world. Dejection is *katepheia* meaning downcast. It is an interesting word because it also has a positive meaning. It comes from *kara*, meaning down from, thought out, according to, and *phaino*, meaning to bring into the light, cause to shine. This suggests that joy, *chara*, from *chairo*, meaning rejoice, can be expressed in a physical way or a spiritual way. The choice is ours.

"Humble yourselves before the Lord and he will exalt you." Being

humble is a misunderstood process. The Greek word for humble is *tapeinoo*, and means to level, to make low, not rising far from the ground. If we take it to mean 'to level' we come back to the balancing of sympathy and antipathy rather than a submissive state of being.

We do this *"before the Lord"*, where 'before' *enopion*, means in the presence, and it is a derivative of behold, to allow one's self to be seen, to appear. The Lord, *kurios*, can be our I Am, our Higher Self. As we connect with our High Self we allow who we really are to be seen. Our true self begins to show itself, it will be exalted.

The rest of this text speaks about the way we conduct our lives when we live life on this earth through an awareness of our Higher Self. We need to be strong and committed while at the same time accepting of others regardless of the way they approach life. This speaks to us of the third and highest level of our spirit which we call Intuition. At this level we can enter into others and experience them. If we can do this would we judge them? Probably not because we can see why they act the way they do.

> *Come now, you who say, "Today or tomorrow we will go into such and such a town and spend a year there and trade and get gain"; whereas you do not know about tomorrow. What is your life? For you are a mist that appears for a little time and then vanishes. Instead you ought to say, "If the Lord wills, we shall live and we shall do this or that." As it is, you boast in your arrogance. All such boasting is evil. Whoever knows what is right to do and fails to do it, for him it is sin. James 4:13-17*

When reading the Bible we should always keep in mind that it is a deep treasure chest of secrets about human development. It preserves spiritual truth in ingenious ways and we can discover this truth if we remain open to various meanings of its words. The first verse speaks of going into a town and spending a year there. Does this mean moving to a new town or city, or does it mean moving to another consciousness?

If it is another consciousness it says that we will do this during the day, *semeron*, not at night. During the day we live on the earth, at night, we lose consciousness of this earth because our astral and I-being leave our physical and etheric bodies in the bed. The text doesn't say, *"we will go into such and such a town"* it says 'we will go into that city'. The word 'go' is *poreuomai*, means to lead over, transfer, depart from life. We can therefore take this to mean to that we go into another consciousness and we do it during the day. This means that while we go about our daily life on this earth, we can go or transfer into our spiritual consciousness of which we are not always aware.

We spend a year there. Spend, *poieo,* means to produce, to prepare, which we do for a year, *eniautos*, which means some fixed or definite period, not necessarily twelve months. During this time we trade, *emporeuomai*, which means to use a person or thing for gain. We also *"get gain"*, *kerdaino*, meaning we acquire, to our advantage. We might wonder why both these words were necessary, perhaps there is an even deeper meaning.

James is saying that it is to our advantage to develop this consciousness if we are to meet tomorrow which we do not know about. Then he asks an important question: *"What is your life?"* the word life is *zoe* which means eternal life and more. There are three words for life: *bios, psuche*, and *zoe*. *Bios* is physical life, *psuche* is soul life, and *zoe* is spiritual life. Zoe is a living force not bound to the physical. If we think about these three expressions of life we know that our physical life, *bios*, has a limited lifespan, our soul life can be semiconscious unless we work on it, and for the most part we are unconscious of our spiritual life. James is asking us to become more conscious of it so that we can answer the question: *"What is your life?"*

Then he says, *"For you are a mist that appears for a little time and then vanishes."* Isn't this a direct reference to reincarnation? Mist, *poios,* means vapor and comes from *aer,* the air, particularly the lower and denser air as distinguished from the higher and rarer air, the atmospheric region. We appear in this region *"for a little time".* The word appear is not in the Greek but the word translated as 'for' is *phaino,* which means to bring forth into the light, cause to shine. So we bring forth our light for a little time and then vanish, *aphanizo,* which means to snatch out of sight, from *aphanes,* meaning not manifest, hidden. Again, we get a sense of the idea of reincarnation.

How do we shine light? We do this through our astral (starry) body, which is part of our soul. As we connect with our I Am, we transform our astral body into a higher soul expression. The more we can do this, the brighter it shines. This involves working consciously with our soul faculties of thinking, feeling, and will.

The next verse says, *"If the Lord wills, we shall live and we shall do this or that."* It doesn't make much sense unless we revert back to the Greek. The Lord, as previously mentioned, usually refers to our Higher Self, our I Am. Live, *zao,* speaks of our spiritual life not our physical life. The words *"do this or that"* do not reveal what is really being said. *"Do"* is *poieo,* the same word translated as 'spend' above. It means to produce, prepare, act, or cause. This gives us a sense of the highest intention, the highest use of our will. The word 'this' is *houtos* and speaks of something near to us. 'That', *ekeino*s from *ekei,* means there, or to that place, and is frequently used as euphemism for 'in another world'. Again we get a sense of engaging in a higher consciousness.

"As it is, you boast in your arrogance. All such boasting is evil."

The word arrogance is not in the Greek. Boasting, *alazoneia*, means to be an empty pretender. This Greek verse says: you rejoice in your pretence, such rejoicing is evil. This gives us a sense of thinking that we understand everything as we live in the physical world without any connection to the spiritual world.

The warning about evil and sin are nothing to feel guilty about. Evil, *poneros*, means worthless, of no value; sin means missing the mark indicating that we can always become a better shot.

CHAPTER 5
JAMES 5

Come now, you rich, weep and howl for the miseries that are coming upon you. Your riches have rotted and your garments are moth-eaten. Your gold and silver have rusted, and their rust will be evidence against you and will eat your flesh like fire. You have laid up treasure for the last days. James 5:1-3

James now emphasizes the importance of seeing our physical life in terms of our spiritual life. Our physical bodies are a veil or a garment covering the reality of our spiritual being. This is how it should be because the physical garment makes us aware of ourselves as individual beings. Without this perspective we are an undifferentiated part of Universe. The purpose of evolution is that we become aware of our full potential as unique individuals who work towards true community with other individuals. This is achieved through experiencing the highest form of love which is identified in the Bible as *agape*.

We cannot fully understand all of this unless we fully understand the principle of reincarnation. This is a challenge while living in a physical body which veils the details about our past lives. We will only be able to see these details when we have developed certain inner principles which today we might call conscience and morality. These principles are also not understood because they are only experienced when our Higher Self, our I Am is connected to our earthly bodies. Conscience, among other things, is an inner revelation of our past lives - we understand our motives. We experience morality when happiness is not acquired at the expense of others.

James' words can be read in a materialistic way, applying them to the human behavior we see in the world today, or we can apply it spiritually to see how our thoughts and feelings lead us astray. James mentions our flesh, *sarx*, which is not our physical body but refers to our astral, our sentient body, that part of us that perceives the things outside us making us aware that we are individuals. The best way to understand this is to think of what happens when we fall asleep; we lose consciousness of the world around us because our astral body leaves our physical (and etheric) body lying there.

Our astral body is our sensuous nature as discussed previously. When we allow it to function instinctively it gets swallowed up in the earthly world and thinks only of itself. We can recognize this in some aspects of animal behavior. Our task is to overcome these self-centered inclinations so that we integrate our Higher Self into our earthly life.

Our ideas of what it means to be rich are skewed; rich, *plousios* means abounding in material resources and comes from the word *ploutos* which refers to external possessions. Why are external possessions valued? If we deeply consider our situation on this earth we come to understand that at the core of our being we are unhappy. This unhappiness is not a weakness; it is prompting us to discover our true strength. Yet often, the slightest awareness of this unhappiness leads many people to seek comfort in material resources. Instead, we must use this awareness to find the strength to connect with our Higher Self. If we can do this, even to a small extent, the happiness we will experience is far greater than the satisfaction that comes from material riches - which are not restricted to possessions but also to materialistic ideas.

The further along we travel in human evolution, the more important it is to understand the true nature of humanity. If we can connect with our Higher Self and begin to see ourselves as spiritual beings that have travelled through this evolution since the time of Adam and Eve, we understand the importance of James' warning. We will see how we are prone to rotting, rusting, and becoming moth-eaten.

What is very important to understand here is that unless we make effort to bring our Higher Self into our lives on this earth, our astral body will deteriorate. As long as we place all our efforts into become earthly rich, and ignore the higher, fourth element of our being, our I-being, our astral body will be consumed by fire. The element of fire belongs to our I-being. In our astral body it will be destructive. It is the element of air that belongs to our astral body. Our task is to develop all four bodies in an orderly way and we do this by connecting with our I-being purposefully and developing all our bodies into their higher expression.

The sign that we are not doing this is when we over-value the resources of the physical world. This means that we do not understand who we really are as spiritual beings with a long history throughout the ages. Riches are not physical possessions gained on this earth in one life; riches are spiritual gifts earned life after life on this earth. And this is the purpose of living repeated lives.

The treasure we must lay up for our last days is the treasure we find deep within us in our I-being. We have been given this gift as individuals and it is our personal task to find it and use it for eternal purposes.

Behold, the wages of the laborers who mowed your fields, which you kept back by fraud, cry out; and the cries of the harvesters have reached the ears of the Lord of hosts. You have lived on the earth in luxury and in pleasure; you have fattened your hearts in a day of slaughter. You have condemned, you have killed the righteous man; he does not resist you. James 5:4-6

Spiritual development requires individual effort, now more than ever before. As we go about our lives each day we need to identify that it is the actual effort behind the work that benefits us, not the outcome. Paying someone else to do this work reveals that the purpose of the work escapes us. James points out what can happen when we are incarnated on this earth without any spiritual view. It is the work to gain this spiritual view that needs to concern our every waking moment.

James is explaining what can take place among many people who take life as it comes without a second thought. He uses the story of an employer and employee, explaining that the result of the work can be claimed by the one who doesn't do it, and that they fraudulently don't pay the full amount for the work done. Sure, we could say that they have worked to earn the money they are using to pay the laborer but the focus here is on their actions and motives.

When a verse begins with the word "Behold" *idou*, we are being directed to look at the spiritual meaning behind the words. This is the esoteric meaning that flows beneath the surface. Behold is a signal to avoid the everyday understanding of words.

The wages, *misthos*, speak of hiring and rewarding the

laborer, *ergates*, the worker and the word *ergates* comes from *ergon*, meaning energy. The word 'mow' is interesting because it speaks of doing something together. This would indicate that we don't simply pay someone to do something for us but we join them in their efforts. But, it is their effort, not ours. Mow is *amao*, meaning reap, mow down, and comes from *hama*, meaning at the same time, together. So often when we pay someone to do something for us, we leave them to do it. How often do we think to accompany them as they do the task? To hold them in our hearts as they do tasks we can't do, or don't have time to do?

What is being mowed here is fields, *chora*, which means the space lying between two places of limits. It comes from *chasma*, which means a chasm, a gulf. This could be speaking about the abyss between this physical world and the spiritual world. Is the laborer being paid to tidy up all that has grown in the abyss because of our inability to attend to our spiritual growth?

When it comes to payment, the full amount is not paid. This does not necessarily mean money; it can mean any kind of recompense. In the Greek, the words "kept back" are not there, it simply says "you defrauded". Fraud is *apostereo* from *apo*, of separation, and *stereo* to deprive. Not only did we not accompany the worker, for example, by holding them in our hearts or in other ways, we then undervalued their efforts. Is this what we do today as we purchase goods? We want the cheapest and we give little thought to those who produced what we buy.

This causes the laborers to cry out so loudly that their cries reach the Lord, *Kurios* of hosts, *sabaoth,* which means armies in Hebrew. These armies are the limitless throng of spiritual beings who guide and guard the harmony of the Universe. If we pay others to do our work for us these beings have to put in greater effort to restore the imbalance our motives and actions cause.

We might ask ourselves how often we think of these beings who work all around us to keep everything in order. Do we consider that they do this for us so that we have every opportunity to do our own work, and in this way contribute to the evolution of the Universe. If we are more mindful of this collective work we will never look to benefit from others, to 'pay' them to do our work for us, and then not 'pay' them fully for their work.

The rest of the text speaks for itself. We seek luxury and pleasure in *"this day of slaughter"*. Slaughter is *sphage*, which means destruction, from *sphazo*, meaning put to death by violence. Is this speaking to us of the crucifixion of Jesus? Verse 6 adds to this *"You have condemned, you have killed the righteous man; he does not resist you."* Isn't this telling us that we must die to this world as Jesus did? He went along with the crucifixion; he didn't resist being nailed to the cross of this world. It could even be pointing out that there are elements within us that need to be put to death, those elements that do not want to do the work, that pay someone else but don't pay them fully. This will apply to our attitudes about others, the way we treat them, as well as the way they respond to us. We will only become aware of this through observing our interactions with others throughout each day.

Be patient, therefore, brethren, until the coming of the Lord. Behold, the farmer waits for the precious fruit of the earth, being patient over it until it receives the early and the late rain. You also be patient. Establish your hearts, for the coming of the Lord is at hand. Do not grumble, brethren, against one another, that you may not be judged; behold, the Judge is standing at the doors. As an example of suffering and patience, brethren, take the prophets who spoke in the name of the Lord. James 5:7-10

What does *"the coming of the Lord"* really mean? Do we automatically think of some external being coming to save us? Is this being called "Lord" referring to Christ Jesus? We should bear in mind that at the time James is writing his letters, the event of the Christen-ing of Jesus has already taken place. James is now preparing us for what will happen within us as we work with this event in our inner lives.

We can easily overlook the word 'coming', yet it is an important word in the Greek, *parousia*. *Parousia* comes from *pareimi* which is derived from *para* meaning from, by, near; and *eimi*, which means 'to be'. This brings us to the Greek term for the I Am - *ego eimi*.

The word Lord, *kurios*, means owner, he to whom a person or thing belongs, about which he has power of deciding. From this we can understand that the Lord, the *kurios*, means our True Self, our I Am. If we look at the text with these ideas in mind it makes a lot of sense. Our I Am is present in all our repeated lives on Earth. It is the precious fruit of the earth for which the farmer patiently waits. The key word is patient, *makrothymeo*, which comes from *makros* which means long, and *thymos* which means passion, strong feeling. Interestingly, the word *thymos* comes from *thyo* which means to sacrifice or kill. This speaks to us of the inner process we experience to express patience.

When we experience the highest form of patience, when we kill all our feelings of impatience, we begin to experience the highest form of love, *agape*. Our I Am can only manifest when our capacity to love embraces everyone and everything in this world, as well as in the spiritual world. This love must be as strong as our own love for ourselves. In other words, we no longer put our own self-interests first, and like the Judge we patiently weigh everything up. This means that we can be truly objective in every facet of our lives. We don't lean towards the things that benefit us because we can see the consequences self-gain has for others.

The only way we can really come to this position is when we live our lives knowing that we have lived other lives on the earth. We also develop objectivity about our actions in past lives. These actions lie at the core of our karma and show us the reasons behind our response to people and events in our current life. We look at this from the position of the objective Judge and through true understanding can remain impartial.

Here lies our challenge in all the moments of our life. It is not only about remaining objective, it is also about recognizing that each interaction with others is founded on interactions in earlier lives. What brings this to our awareness? Our conscious connection with our I Am. This is why we have to work hard to forge this connection. If it could be done hastily we may not be able to bear seeing what we have done in our past lives.

"Do not grumble", *stenazo*, which means to sigh or groan, a word that comes from *stenos* meaning narrow. We always grumble when our view is narrow. The urge to grumble about others is a signal to us that we are dealing with karma. It is also a signal to be patient and forgiving. The degree to which we can be patient tells us about the extent to which we are connected to our Higher Self, our I Am. The groan that rises up within us sparks the inner work we must do if we are to remain objective.

James then gives this advice: *"As an example of suffering and patience, brethren, take the prophets who spoke in the name of the Lord."*

The word suffering is *kakopatheia*, and means suffering of evil. It comes from *kakos*, meaning bad nature, wrong, or destructive; and *pathos*, meaning whatever befalls one, sad or joyous, good or bad. This speaks to us of our destiny. It also suggests that we shouldn't get carried away with either good or bad events in our lives. Karma is not just about difficulties, it also includes what is enjoyable in our lives. We can often get carried away with what we enjoy and not see what is behind the gift of enjoyment.

Then we can ask why James uses the prophets as an example. Prophets, *prophetes* are the ones who interpret hidden things (like karma). These prophets spoke in the name of the Lord, *kurios*, the Higher Self, our I Am. Again we have confirmation of the things that remain hidden in our Higher Self until we have the patience and objectivity to see them.

> *Behold, we call those happy who were steadfast. You have heard of the steadfastness of Job, and you have seen the purpose of the Lord, how the Lord is compassionate and merciful. But above all, my brethren, do not swear, either by heaven or by earth or with any other oath, but let your yes be yes and your no be no, that you may not fall under condemnation. James 5:11-12*

Again we are asked to behold, to look for the hidden meaning behind the words. Happy doesn't really give us a sense of the Greek word *makarizo*, which really means blessed, we could say a large happy blessing. The state of happiness is worth contemplating because often it points to escapism. We look for ways to escape situations that make us unhappy. Instead, we should look for ways to overcome our challenges and not just laugh them off. Blessed speaks of a resting place, a place where we can be calm even under the greatest challenge. When we achieve this we are lead to a state of being steadfast. Steadfast is *hypomeno*, which means to abide, to remain in place instead of leaving, to endure till the end - it also speaks of suffering.

This is why Job is given as an example. Job was a wealthy man severely tested by Satan but always remained true to God. He was an example of endurance. Job remained steadfast because of his patience, *hypomone*, which means to remain. This is a patience that is achieved through trials. We remain unmoved, our goal is strong, and we gain strength from the experience. In this way we see the purpose of the Lord. Purpose, *telos*, means end, termination, the limit at which a thing ceases to be. It speaks of the end of some act or state of being rather than an end of a period of time. If we think of the Lord as our I Am then we can understand that the testing is to strengthen us so that we can work with the power of our I Am more closely. We can only do this if we strive to understand the nature of our I Am. Often, the only way to do this is to see the work of Satan in our lives. We don't have to succumb to him; we only need to see his work. These tests are ongoing, but each one comes to an end when we understand it.

James reminds us that the Lord, our I Am, is *"compassionate and merciful."* When we face our challenges we need to remind ourselves of their higher purpose. Compassionate is *polysplanchnos* which means full of pity, very kind. Merciful, *oiktirmon,* comes from *oikteiro* meaning to pity, to have compassion. While these words seem similar we can understand that *polysplanchnos* is personal inner feeling, while *oiktirmon* is about feeling for the other person, experiencing their distress as if it was our own. These experiences come to us through our I Am, and when we are strong enough to experience them we know that we are on purpose.

The next verse is one of the highest principles in life, *"let your yes be yes and your no be no."* How often do we say yes and not really mean it, and how often are afraid to say no? This is a question of commitment and it requires great strength. We can only have this kind of strength when we work through our I Am. If we remain in the lower parts of our soul we tend to say what we think others want to hear. This is mainly because we don't have the courage to deal with the responses we get, especially when we say no. It can be very isolating. Yet, if we say what we think is expected of us are our relationships genuine?

When we make a true commitment, when we confidently say yes or no to situations, we begin to build the true community that rises from those who express themselves through their I Am. At first we may stand alone, but gradually those who manage to do the same will join us. James tells us that there are two kinds of people, those who do not fall, and those who do. Fall is *pipto,* meaning to descend from a higher place to a lower place. The words *"under condemnation"* are not in the Greek. The word translated as condemnation is *krisis.* James is saying that if we have the strength to remain genuine, if we can say yes and no when we mean it, we will avoid the *krisis* fall. *Krisis* means judgment which is a process of assessment and means separating (analyzing) the facts before a decision is made.

Each life on this earth gives us the opportunity to express ourselves individually. This means that we make personal decisions based on what we understand of each situation we are in. We have the strength to do this through our Higher Self and when we rely on the opinions of others we know that our Higher Self has stepped back. Not that this is a bad thing because our life is a testing ground, we live in a continual state of judgment which brings us closer and closer to our I Am and our true community.

Is any one among you suffering? Let him pray. Is any cheerful? Let him sing praise. Is any among you sick? Let him call for the elders of the church, and let them pray over him, anointing him with oil in the name of the Lord; and the prayer of faith will save the sick man, and the Lord will raise him up; and if he has committed sins, he will be forgiven. Therefore confess your sins to one another, and pray for one another, that you may be healed. The prayer of a righteous man has great power in its effects. James 5:13-16

What is suffering? Suffering in Greek is *kakopatheo*, which comes from two words; *kakos* which means of a bad nature, a nature not as it ought to be; and *patheo* which means whatever befalls us. We know that living on this earth without spiritual insight is not as it ought to be. Unless we strive for spiritual insight we will have 'a bad nature'. We are called to recognize this condition and pray.

The advice to pray could be taken in two ways. One way is to divest ourselves of all responsibility for the situation we are in; the other way is to take responsibility and act according to the situation we find ourselves in. Prayer does not mean to beg for help. Prayer means to focus our energy and align ourselves with our purpose. Then we can admit that we recognize our 'bad nature' and seek to understand why this is, and then look for ways to overcome it. It also means to make a commitment and to state this commitment to the Universe and all the spiritual beings contained in it. When we come to this point we will receive assistance. This assistance may come from our Guardian Angel or even higher beings.

James then asks, "Is any cheerful?" Cheerful is *euthymeo* and means to be in good spirits, if so, then we can sing (there is no mention of praise). Sing is *psallo* which means to vibrate, as the strings of an instrument vibrate when it is played. This could be speaking to us of our chakras, the lotus flowers or spiritual centers in our body. These centers vibrate according to our inner energy. We are more energetic and peaceful when the energy flows freely.

The energy of these chakras changes as we understand higher knowledge and connect with our I Am. As these spiritual centers are the sense-organs of our soul they tell us a lot about the subtler things in life. We begin to see more clearly into our soul and understand ourselves more deeply. If we are sick, *astheneo*, which means weak, pointing to a weakness of soul, this requires compassion for ourselves. Those who have this deep compassion could be referred to as the "elders of the church" who anoint, *aleipho*, which means to give a healthy look to the skin. In other words, we begin to shine with spirit. Our inner light makes our skin glow. Then we know we have been anointed in the name of the Lord, anointed by our connection with our I Am.

Then we have the ability to pray with faith. Faith *pistis*, doesn't mean to have blind belief, when we have faith we have knowledge, understanding. Then the sick (man does not appear in the Greek) will be saved. To be saved means to keep safe from those forces that seek to distract us from the path. This second mention of the word sick is *kamno* which means to grow weary. When we sense this weariness within us we can be confident that our Higher Self is poised to raise us up. The word raise is *egeiro* and means to arouse, like arousing from sleep. What we need to understand is that life on the earth is a kind of sleep. We are asleep to the spiritual worlds and we are asleep to our I Am. The arousing is like the princess kissing the frog to awaken the prince within.

In this awakening sins will be revealed. Not only that, but the reasons behind these sins will become obvious, they are part of our karma, and our karma has great purpose in our life. Sin, *hamartia*, means missing the mark and we can't hit the bullseye when we can't see the spiritual reality in which we live. These sins will be forgiven, *aphiemi*, which means to send away. Again, the Bible text suggests that someone or something else will forgive us. This is not the case; we will forgive ourselves for missing the mark and in this way see the target so that we sharpen our aim.

Once we understand our karma, our purpose for incarnating on the earth, we can discuss this with others. We can confess *exomologeo*, from *homologeo* which means to declare openly and to agree. Now, the word used for sin is *paraptoma*, which means to fall beside, to deviate from the path. In our openness, without judgment, we can pray together, we can focus our energy and align ourselves with our purpose. This has more power, *energeo*, when we share it with others. We become righteous, *dikaios,* which means we make a continual series of adjustments which restores balance and harmony within us. Then we are healed, made whole, not through something outside us but through our own inner work which is then witnessed by those around us.

Eli'jah was a man of like nature with ourselves and he prayed fervently that it might not rain, and for three years and six months it did not rain on the earth. Then he prayed again and the heaven gave rain, and the earth brought forth its fruit. My brethren, if any one among you wanders from the truth and some one brings him back, let him know that whoever brings back a sinner from the error of his way will save his soul from death and will cover a multitude of sins. James 5:17-20

Why would Elijah pray for no rain? Rain can point to the growth of plants to produce food, and water to drink, to sustain the physical body on this earth. Rain or moisture can also represent ideas coming from above. Why three and half years? The time period of three and half years is significant in terms of evolution which takes place in stages of seven. The first stages focus on development or evolution, the middle stages bring forth the fruit, and the last stages are the decline or involution which prepares for the next seven stages.

It is very important for us to understand evolution, yet it is hard to grasp what it means because it happens over such a long period of time. We must start with the idea of reincarnation and at the same time understand that we are not just physical beings. We are beings of soul and spirit who take up a physical body on this earth from time to time. If we do not understand this we are sinners, we miss the mark.

This raises the question of purpose. What is the purpose of evolution and repeated lives on the earth? At this time in our evolution we can only answer this question if we look to the I Am. A literal translation of the first verse reads like this "Elijah a man to be (*ego*) similarly affected as I am (*eimi*)" Isn't this telling us that Elijah had developed his connection with his I Am? This is very significant because human beings have only been able to develop this connection since Christ entered the body of Jesus, and Elijah lived long before the Christ event.

We could interpret the second verse, *"when the heaven gave rain"*, as the coming of Christ. The real fruit of this earth is sustained by the presence of Christ in the physical earth, in the etheric of the earth and within us, in our blood. We actually produce the fruit as we awaken the presence of Christ within us. This is the truth, *aletheia*, which means un-hidden, not forgetting, not losing. In essence it means un-forgetting. As we live in our physical bodies on the earth we have forgotten who we are and where we were before we were born. Only when we connect with our I Am will we un-forget this information. Only when we have a developed spiritual fortitude will we be able to withstand the impact of seeing who we were in past lives. This requires a high level of objectivity.

Then James speaks about bringing a sinner back from his sins. This is one of the most misunderstood ideas on this earth. The idea of correcting others, of acting outwardly instead of having inner actions which change ourselves, is prevalent everywhere. Often those who seek to change others, to point out where they go wrong, are themselves missing the mark. It is as if they get some relief from their own sins by pointing out the sins of others. Yet, this simply makes matters worse.

Indeed, when James says, *"whoever brings back a sinner from the error"* he isn't necessarily meaning that the sinner is someone else, it could be ourselves. Again, this requires a level of objectivity to assess the ways in which we miss the mark. How do address our own sinfulness? Certainly not by reliving it and beating ourselves up about it.

James stresses the importance of this by saying that this activity *"will save his soul from death"*. Death, *thanatos*, is a word that comes from *thnesko*, which means spiritually dead. We can then ask ourselves how we stay spiritually alive. We live on this earth, we cannot see the full picture, and yet we are called continually to strive to understand that which we cannot fully see. The rain has stopped because of Elijah's actions - he prayed for it not to rain. The lack of rain prevented the production of fruit.

If we then think about Elijah as the one connected with the I Am long before human beings on the earth could have a personal connection with their I Am, we can ask deeper questions about his purpose. Does the lack of rain, which delays the production of fruit, mean that it is important for there to be a delay in human beings ability to have a personal experience of their I Am?

James knows this to be true and he says that awareness of sins brings new life and *"will cover a multitude of sins."* Cover, *kalypto*, means hide, veil, hinder the knowledge of a thing. We can now see the dangers in this knowledge. If we think our sins can be covered at some time in the future we may not worry about sinning in the present. Each of us is called to take up the responsibility of seeing our sins, and in so doing we will not repeat them. It is this insight that saves our soul from spiritual death.

CHAPTER 6
THE FIRST LETTER OF PETER
PETER 1

Peter, an apostle of Jesus Christ, To the exiles of the Dispersion in Pontus, Galatia, Cappado'cia, Asia, and Bithyn'ia, chosen and destined by God the Father and sanctified by the Spirit for obedience to Jesus Christ and for sprinkling with his blood: May grace and peace be multiplied to you. Blessed be the God and Father of our Lord Jesus Christ! By his great mercy we have been born anew to a living hope through the resurrection of Jesus Christ from the dead, and to an inheritance which is imperishable, undefiled, and unfading, kept in heaven for you, who by God's power are guarded through faith for a salvation ready to be revealed in the last time. 1 Peter 1:1-5

Peter's view is different from James' view, which is only natural, as each of us will have a different view according to our own deliberations. This is an important point to consider in a world intent on agreeing to one view. We can only move forward on our journey by remaining open to assessing each new view.

Knowing who Peter is helps us understand his message. His name was Simon Peter: Simon means hearing and Peter means faith. He captures the essence of our ability to hear and see spiritually. Our faith becomes knowingness, not a blind faith. (see "The Twelve Disciples in the Gospel of St John" by Kristina Kaine on Amazon.)

Peter states that he speaks to people from specific locations, saying that they are chosen. If we take this on face value it seems quite limiting, but if we look at the deeper meaning that these places represent it may give us a broader view. These people are exiles, indicating that they have gone to a foreign country, which can mean that their consciousness has changed. They are exiles of the dispersion, the diaspora, which tells us that they have scattered; not only have they left the group consciousness they lived in, they have also begun to develop their own understanding of what has taken place with the crucifixion and resurrection of Christ Jesus. At the time of this event, many people would not have been aware of it.

The regions Peter mentions can be taken to represent different kinds of consciousness. Charles Fillmore's Metaphysical Bible Dictionary gives some ideas about what these regions point to in the development of our consciousness. Pontus means "the sea", a deep body of water, and can represent the universal mind. This takes us away from the limited group consciousness of our town and helps us understand things from the perspective of humanity as a whole. Galatia means "white as milk" and points to pure, simple truths. Cappadocia means "province of good horses" indicating the union in consciousness with the substance (pastures) of life where strength and vitality are sustained.

Asia, "orient" indicates the inner, source of spirit, which will now be developed into something new, and Bithynia, which means "a violent rushing", speaks of the movement of our spiritual energy, our Kundalini, from the base of our spine.

Then Peter speaks of the blessing that has been given to those people who have broken away from the group consciousness they have lived in for some time. These words call to those of us who seek a deeper understanding of the pivotal event that Jesus experienced as he took into himself the Cosmic Christ. Peter's words assure us that we will be changed, "born anew", and that we will be supported in our efforts to take on this new consciousness. The living hope *zao elpis,* has a special meaning. *Zao* means the spiritualized life force, or etheric force imbued with our own I Am. When Peter spoke about this activity of the I Am it would have shocked many people. Humanity had lived with the group I Am, held by Jehovah until the time of Christ, now each person could claim their individual I Am.

The inheritance was received: "an inheritance which is imperishable, undefiled, and unfading, kept in heaven for you," This is a direct reference to the I Am which is eternal. When we connect with our I Am we connect with eternity. We step out of our individual incarnations into eternal life which alters our whole existence. We start expressing ourselves through all the lifetimes we have lived on the earth, and all that we experience between these lives in the spiritual worlds. This means that we have an enormous influence; our words and deeds are freed from this one incarnation and echo down the ages and forever. This inheritance calls us to deeply consider what this means for us in this life.

Peters says that this inheritance is *"kept in heaven for you"*; kept is *tereo* means to attend to carefully, to guard, to watch. Heaven, *ouranos,* means the idea of elevation, the same idea as *oros* meaning mountain. This is not a place 'up there somewhere', it is all that is elevated within us. It is kept apart from our lower, earthly expressions in daily life. Yet, at any time we can include the heavenly in our lives.

As we work with these principles Peter tells us that we, "by God's power are guarded through faith for a salvation ready to be revealed in the last time." This power is *dunamis* associated with those beings in the Spiritual Hierarchy who lead and guide movement. The movement from group to individual expression of the I Am is a huge movement of power. We can understand the need to be guarded as this transition takes place. There are many beings in the Universe keen to prevent this from happening because it will give human beings incredible power. Our task is to align ourselves with the highest so that we can contribute to this mighty plan to be revealed, *apokalypto* - the apocalypse.

In this you rejoice, though now for a little while you may have to suffer various trials, so that the genuineness of your faith, more precious than gold which though perishable is tested by fire, may redound to praise and glory and honor at the revelation of Jesus Christ. Without having seen him you love him; though you do not now see him you believe in him and rejoice with unutterable and exalted joy. As the outcome of your faith you obtain the salvation of your souls. 1 Peter 1:6-9

Peter points out that we have work to do, and if we do this work we will be highly rewarded. The rewards are to be believed but again, not blindly. Faith is not blind, faith, *pistis*, is a real experience that we create for ourselves. This entails creating a real experience of the Christ-ening of Jesus written about in the New Testament from so many aspects.

Those who have been involved in, and informed by, religious groups in this life often have a very superficial understanding of Jesus and Christ. Understanding in depth the journey Jesus made to the cross, and the ways in which the Cosmic being called Christ was able to enter into his body, releases us from the misguided ideas of modern religion. We could say that these represent some of the various trials we have to suffer.

The Greek meaning of suffer is perhaps a little different from our modern understanding. Suffer is *lypeo,* which means to make sorrowful and comes from the word *lype*, which means sorrow, pain, and grief. Now that we are able to integrate the highest human element into our being, the powerful I Am, we will grieve the loss of the life we previously lived. This life, to a large extent, is not conscious. We know this by becoming aware of the many things we do during the day without thinking. As we become more conscious of our motives we begin to feel sorrow, pain, and grief. By understanding this our suffering becomes more bearable.

The *"various trials"* may not be what first come to mind. The Greek word for various is *poikilos,* which means various colors, variegated. Our whole being is infused with various colors, which can be called our aura. The colors of this aura are influenced by our past lives, as well as the way we live our present life. As we integrate our I Am and awaken the presence of Christ within us, these colors change. As these colors change so does our personality and outlook on life. We know that change can be difficult and sometimes painful and so these changes can be referred to as trials.

Trials, *peirasmos,* means experiments and comes from the Greek *peirazo*, which means to endeavor, to try whether a thing can be done. It points to working out what we think and feel, or how we will behave, in a good or bad sense. This is not something imposed on us; it comes from within us as we awaken our consciousness. It is about experimenting with our approach to life and we work with this through the years to achieve our highest goals.

This tests the *"genuineness of your faith."* Genuineness is *dokimion* which means proving or approved. The most important thing for us to approve of, or accept, is our belief in our I Am and the presence of Christ within us. When we are committed to this work, the inner presence of Christ will give us assurances that we are on the right track. We don't blindly accept this, we continually test it; as Peter says, it is "tested by fire". The fire within us is our I Am, it resides in our blood which is responsible for our body's temperature.

Peter says that this testing will redound, *heurisko*, which means to discover, to find by enquiry. So we will always be inquiring of our inner discoveries and our understanding will be strengthened. This is quite a different experience to the one which accepts something once and leaves it at that. The ongoing testing is like climbing a steep mountain and each step we take is tested for its ability to hold our weight.

This activity is supported when we are able to do as Peter says, *"Without having seen him you love him"*. We should not underestimate the power that is generated within us as we reinforce our love for Christ Jesus. As this love grows we begin to see him. Rev Mario Schoenmaker spoke of this in 1996.

"I believe that you cannot love the Christ properly without having seen him. I think I have said that before. If you create within your soul a picture of the Christ in accordance to your own imagination, hold that picture before you in your brain when you contemplate, then you will find that your love becomes stronger.

The wonder of the Christ spirit is that he is not fastened to a particular manifestation. So even if you create that picture within your consciousness with all the beauty you can give it - and each picture from each person can be different and probably is - the manifestation of the Christ is not limited. He manifests himself through the picture that you create. Then you start loving him better, deeper, greater. Then your devotions are no longer a duty, then they are a joy. Then your prayers are a deep need for communication, then your love will be extended and become manifest in all areas of your life." Rev Mario Schoenmaker

The prophets who prophesied of the grace that was to be yours searched and inquired about this salvation; they inquired what person or time was indicated by the Spirit of Christ within them when predicting the sufferings of Christ and the subsequent glory. It was revealed to them that they were serving not themselves but you, in the things which have now been announced to you by those who preached the good news to you through the Holy Spirit sent from heaven, things into which angels long to look. Therefore gird up your minds, be sober, set your hope fully upon the grace that is coming to you at the revelation of Jesus Christ. 1 Peter 1:10-13

Now Peter speaks of things that can't be easily understood. He is calling us to trust in the future, again not blindly, but to listen, to open ourselves to predictions. In this sense, Peter himself is being a prophet. The word prophet in the Greek is *prophetes* which is a compound of *pro*, meaning before, and *phemi*, meaning to make known one's thoughts, to declare them. The prophets are the ones who understand things earlier than others do. They are those who can make these thoughts, not only known, but also understood.

These prophets who saw things early now speak about grace. James spoke about grace and it is something we should think about deeply. We looked into this earlier. "Grace, *charis,* is what we experience in the second level of our spirit, our Life Spirit. When we begin to use this second level of spirit we experience Inspiration, the images that we created though spiritual Imagination [the first level of our spirit] start to breathe into us, to speak to us. Grace is also the ability to have full control over all our feelings, thoughts, and actions. It is the ability to see God, or the highest, in everyone and everything. Then all our responses are graceful." From James 4:5-8

Of these people who hear the mysteries before many others Peter says they *"searched and enquired about salvation"* Search is *exereunao* which means to seek in order to find through thinking, meditating or reasoning. Enquired is *ekzeteo* meaning to seek out, investigate, even to beg or crave (for meaning). It comes from two Greek words, *ek* meaning from, *zeteo*, meaning out of. While these two words are similar in meaning, they are two different activities for us to engage in if we want to understand what the prophets see so that we can experience salvation. These two activities are to seek as well as to find.

Salvation, *soteria*, is the feminine version of savior - the deliverer, the preserver. We might wonder why this word takes a feminine perspective. The feminine is more receptive and nurturing while the masculine is more active and individualistic.

Then Peter speaks about Christ within us as we become prophets, he says, *"indicated by the Spirit of Christ within them"*. This idea was spoken of in Colossians 1:27 *"To them God chose to make known how great among the Gentiles are the riches of the glory of this mystery, which is Christ in you, the hope of glory."*

What does it mean to become aware of Christ within us? This is not a personal matter; it means Christ is within everyone.

Then he says that these ones are *"predicting the sufferings of Christ and the subsequent glory."* Predicting, *promartyromai*, means to testify beforehand. This word comes from *pro* meaning before, and *martyromai*, meaning to cite or bring forward a witness. Who is this witness we might ask? Could it be us as we see the deed of Christ in its true meaning and significance when we become aware of Christ within?

Do we then experience Christ's sufferings? Suffering is *pathema* from the Greek word *pathos*, which means whatever befalls one. This is speaking of destiny and, of course, karma. Rudolf Steiner puts the right perspective on destiny with these words.

"The fact that our destiny, our karma, meets us in the form of absolute necessity is no obstacle to our freedom. For when we act, we approach this destiny with the measure of independence we have achieved. It is not destiny that acts, but it is we who act in accordance with the laws of this destiny." How Karma Works - article written in 1903 for Lucifer Gnosis

Then we can understand the *"subsequent glory"* the *doxa*. We looked at the meaning of *doxa* previously. "Glory, *doxa*, means glorified, shining like a star. The star within us is our astral and when we can override its instinctual behavior our light shines. This happens when we purify our soul of its bias and allow ourselves to bring to life the inner experience of what we see." James 2:1-4

Finally, the idea of communication from the spiritual worlds is emphasized in three words: "announced", "gospel", and "angel". Each one speaks of angels, messengers. Announced, *anangello*, from *ana*, into the midst, among, and *angelos*, messenger. Gospel, *euangelizo*, to bring good news from *eu*, to be well off, prosper, and *angelos*, messenger, angel. And the *"things into which angels long to look"*. This last statement means that human beings are actually higher beings than angels - this is another thing we should contemplate deeply.

Therefore we are to gird our minds; the Greek says 'gird the loins of your mind'. Gird is *anazonnymi*, which means prepare, and loins, *osphys* means the hips. The Hebrews thought generative power resided in the hips. The mind, *dianoia*, means thinking through. To be sober, *nepho*, means to be free of intoxicants, to be watchful, calm. Intoxicants can mean intoxicating spiritual experiences which prevent ideas from being thought through. Then we are told that we will only see the revelation, *apokalypto* - the apocalypse, when we experience grace.

As obedient children, do not be conformed to the passions of your former ignorance, but as he who called you is holy, be holy yourselves in all your conduct; since it is written, "You shall be holy, for I am holy." And if you invoke as Father him who judges each one impartially according to his deeds, conduct yourselves with fear throughout the time of your exile. You know that you were ransomed from the futile ways inherited from your fathers, not with perishable things such as silver or gold, but with the precious blood of Christ, like that of a lamb without blemish or spot. 1 Peter 1:14-19

Why does Peter refer to us obedient children? If we explore the words for child then the idea of obedience will make more sense. There are nine different words used in the Bible to refer to the different states of a child. Peter uses *teknon* which is similar to the word *tiko* meaning to beget (produce), to bear. This suggests that the state of the child within us is something we produce.

It is interesting to note that one of the Greek words used to describe the state of the child is *monogenes*. We find this word in the last verse, verse 14, of the Prologue of St John's Gospel. *"we have beheld his glory, glory as of the only Son from the Father."* The word *monogenes* is translated as "only son" misconstruing what is being said. The word 'son' is not in the Greek. *Monogen*es means one-born or self-born. We can ask: what are we self-birthing? Because of the event of Christ entering into Jesus we have been enabled to give birth to our I Am, our eternal self. At the same time we are children of our I Am. Our I Am has given birth to the aspect of itself that we are in this lifetime.

Considering the state of being a child has much to reveal. Rather than think of children as being in a state of immaturity, we can think of their purity and openness, and their willingness to produce something new. What does it mean to be obedient children of our I Am? Obedient, *hypakoe,* means compliance, submission; it comes from the word *hypakouo*; to listen, to harken, to obey. We are called to listen to our I Am, our Higher Self, to discover what it has planned for this life we live on this earth. If we are not able to listen to our I Am then our lives are ad hoc. This is living from *"passions of your former ignorance"* when we were not aware of the role of our I Am in our lives.

Passions, *epithymia*, are not so much passions but a desire, longing, which comes from the word *epithymeo*, meaning those who seek things forbidden. In one sense, access to our I Am is forbidden until we have prepared ourselves. We should note that a strong desire of any kind may be refined in character, but it is evil if not consistent with higher life.

Then Peter says, *"but as he who called you is holy, be holy yourselves in all your conduct;"* We can ask who has called us? Called *kaleo*, means to call aloud, which is similar to the base of *keleuo*, meaning to command, to order. Again, the need to listen is stressed.

What does it mean to be holy? Holy, is *hagios*, from *hagos*, meaning an awful thing, a thing that fills us with awe. This speaks to us again about purity. This purity must manifest in all our conduct. The Greek word for conduct is *anastrophe*, meaning behavior, coming from *anastrepho,* meaning to turn upside down, to overturn, to turn back. This would mean that by turning back to our Higher Self, which determined our present life, we become holy. Peter states it very plainly. "You shall be holy, for I am (*ego eimi*) holy." How often do we think of our I Am as holy?

Peter then introduced the Father principle and speaks of our exile - which is a way of looking at our life on this earth away from the full expression of our I Am. If we see our life on this earth as a birth set in motion by the Father then we can also assume that the Father is our I Am. This I Am

Father is the one who creates the child and provides parental care. We are reassured that this father judges us impartially as we sojourn on the earth and struggle to find our true purpose.

Peter then says, *"You know that you were ransomed from the futile ways inherited from your fathers"*. The use of 'fathers' here could mean ancestors who had no opportunity to connect with their true father, their I Am, until Jesus was able to take the Christ into himself. Ransomed is *lytroo*, which means to release on receipt of ransom, to redeem, to liberate. We pay this ransom ourselves through the way we live our lives on this earth.

For all these reasons we should hold in our hearts the *"precious blood of Christ"*. How often do we think of this blood, *haima*, the seat of life, as the prime reason for our independence and individuality? We feel the impulse of independence all through the day as we resist being reliant on others, when we say to ourselves, "I'll do it my way!" Yet, do we acknowledge the deed of Christ for our ability to think this and express it in our lives?

He was destined before the foundation of the world but was made manifest at the end of the times for your sake. Through him you have confidence in God, who raised him from the dead and gave him glory, so that your faith and hope are in God. Having purified your souls by your obedience to the truth for a sincere love of the brethren, love one another earnestly from the heart. **1 Peter 1:20-22**

The previous verse, 19, says that we were ransomed *"with the precious blood of Christ, like that of a lamb without blemish or spot."* The precious blood of Christ released us from a condition we have had since *"before the foundation of the world"*. What is this condition? And why would we have it?

One answer - and we should not limit ourselves to one answer - is that this condition held us in unity with the whole universe. We could not be individuals in this state. Only when Christ *"could be made manifest"* by entering into the body of Jesus, so becoming the prototype for the true, fully human being, was it possible for us to become individuals.

The word 'destined' has an interesting place in the Greek language. It is *proginosko*, which means to have knowledge beforehand, to foreknow, and the word *ginosko* is the Jewish idiom for sexual intercourse. The word foundation continues along these lines. Foundation, *katabole,* means throwing or laying down. It also refers to the injection or depositing of the virile semen in the womb, or of the seed of plants and animals.

This gives us an idea of the process of Christ entering into us. It is an inseminating and germinating process and we will eventually give birth to the inner presence of Christ. It is hard to imagine that this was set in place before the foundation of the world, the Cosmos. Foundation also means a founding (laying down a foundation) and comes from the word *kataballo* which means to cast down, to put in a lower place. We need to think about these processes in detail because they describe what takes place in our own consciousness as we participate in the process of human development.

It is interesting to think that the Christ event was destined eons ago but could only be made manifest *"at the end of the times for your sake."* Manifest, *phaneroo*, means to make visible or known what has been hidden or unknown. Why could we not know about the plan earlier? This is a burning question, the answer to which can be applied to even the smallest events in our lives. Our task is to go through the processes of growth; these are the experiences which awaken the presence of Christ within us. We know that we do not fully understand situations unless we experience them firsthand. Often, when we describe an experience to a friend, we say, "You had to be there."

The Christ event, which Peter briefly summarizes, is not only a conception but also a death. We must think deeply about these details. We know that one of the most painful experiences in earthly life is death. This could be the death of a person, but it could also be the death of a relationship or even our ideas. Only when we can see death as a step in the process will we receive its full benefit.

This leads us to the idea of faith and hope. As we begin to have an experience of the evolution of humanity and understand that our individual effort will bring us to our predestined potential, our faith grows. As we have previously considered, *"faith pistis, doesn't mean to believe blindly, it speaks of the experience of ginosko, of fully entering into the matter. Faith is actually a clairvoyant power which sees behind the physical, it is a foreseeing knowledge not a substitute for knowledge."*

We must build our confidence in these inner processes of our developing consciousness. It is only when we do this that we can have confidence in our ability to navigate evolution. We will certainly be challenged, especially if we do not engage in the experience of purifying our souls, our *psyche*.

While we might be drawn to look at the big picture of evolution that Peter describes, we always need to apply these ideas in the moment, in our own consciousness. We use our soul in every moment of the day as we feel, think and act. By directing our attention to become more conscious of every feeling, thought and intention we will purify our soul. This is an ongoing process; it is not about success or failure.

At the heart of this effort is love. This love is of the highest nature, *agape*. It is not the kind of love we feel for our partner, our family, or our nation, it is a spiritual love. This love rises above the polarity we experience in our soul as we prefer one person over another. This love connects with the potential in every person. When this potential is met with the highest love it is stirred into action. There is no need for it to be acknowledged. This is a silent and private moment between two people and its effects radiate into the future.

You have been born anew, not of perishable seed but of imperishable, through the living and abiding word of God; for "All flesh is like grass and all its glory like the flower of grass. The grass withers, and the flower falls, but the word of the Lord abides for ever." That word is the good news which was preached to you. 1 Peter 1:23-25

We encounter the Word, the *logos*, again. This is a principal that we can hardly understand with our present mind. Peter refers to it as the *"the living and abiding word of God;"*. In verse 25 he refers to the word again saying, *"the word of the Lord abides for ever."* and *"That word is the good news"*. This time he is not speaking about the *logos* but of *rhema*, which means that which has been uttered, speech, any sound produced by the voice and having definite meaning. Understanding the difference between these two words is fundamental to our spiritual progress. We could say that *logos* is in a non-spoken state while *rhema* spoken.

We looked at some aspects of the *logos* in James' Letter and we can add to that by considering some of the insights of Ernst Katz in his book Core Anthroposophy. He refers to *logos* as the primeval ordering principle. He points to St John's Gospel which starts with the words, *"In the beginning,"* and says that this means, *"when time became distinct from timeless chaos"*.

The idea of becoming *"born anew"* is a similar process. As we live on this earth in a physical body we live in a perishable state; perishable is *phthartos* meaning corruptible, perishing. If we are born anew we enter into an imperishable state, or an eternal state. Georg Kuhlewind, in his book "Becoming Aware of the Logos" explains that *"Eternal life is living consciousness of the I-am-here, which no longer needs to support itself upon the body."* p80 This tells us that we can experience eternity while living in our physical body on this earth but without depending on it. We do this through our awareness of our I Am. Our I Am becomes the supporting structure for life on earth.

We could also say that the Logos has the idea of the I Am which first came to expression through the life of Jesus as he took into himself the Christ Being. The same will happen to us as we replicate this process. Although it will be easier for us now that Jesus has done it.

Ernst Katz explains that *"the Word imparted existence [...] Nothing could become existent unless existence was imparted to it by the Word."* We could think about this principle by considering the example of the seed, *spora*, from *speiro*, meaning to sow, scatter, seed. Our eternal being is seeded within us and must be nurtured to sprout through our own diligence.

At the same time it is important for us to understand that our flesh, our body, is a temporary state. This will only become a reality for us when are able to experience our soul and spirit as the aspects of our being that take on a body from time to time. Only when we can do this are we born anew, *anagennao*, meaning to be born again; from *ana*, amidst, among, and *gennao* to be born. We are born amidst or among ourselves. This gives us the idea of our soul and spirit being born among our flesh. Then we are truly living, *zao*, which means not to be in a state of lifelessness which we are when we think we are only a body of flesh.

If we can grasp some of the meaning of the Logos as first ordering principle, and if we see 'ordering' as alignment of body, soul, and spirit, we will be reborn. If we don't do this we live in chaos. Chaos is a state of disorder and confusion. It means we can't make sense of things, our perceptions are confused, and we are never sure about what is right and wrong. This is why some things that we think are wrong are actually right and vice versa. It is as if this state of chaos is waiting for us to set it in order. Ernst Katz suggests that this is the case.

"Thus the opening words of Saint John's gospel can be interpreted as an attempt to penetrate to the most primary, most encompassing ordering principle that enables us to lift all "things" out of cosmic chaos as well as out of perceptual chaos."

The first 14 verses of St John's gospel are key to spiritual development. We should learn them, say them every day, and perhaps keep a diary of the different meanings that come to us. Then we will be self-born as St John explains in the final verse.

"And the Word became flesh and dwelt among us, full of grace and truth; we have beheld his glory, glory as of the only Son from the Father." John 1:14

As we previously considered, *"The word monogenes is translated as 'only son' misconstruing what is being said. The word 'son' is not in the Greek. Monogenes means one-born or self-born."* Glory of the self-born from the Father. The Father, our progenitor or originator, can be our I Am.

CHAPTER 7
I PETER 2

So put away all malice and all guile and insincerity and envy and all slander. Like newborn babes, long for the pure spiritual milk, that by it you may grow up to salvation; for you have tasted the kindness of the Lord.
I Peter 2:1-3

As we awaken our Higher Self, our I Am, in our consciousness, we become aware of the activity in our soul which has expressed itself unconsciously till now. Peter specifically lists this activity as malice, guile, insincerity, envy, and slander.

Malice is *kakia*, the desire to injure, from *kakos*, to be of a bad nature. Guile, *dolos*, means deceit, a bait, to snare. Insincerity, *hypokrisis*, is hypocrisy, which literally means an answering and points to the ways we act in pretense. Envy, *phthonos*, means to be jealous, and slander, *katalalia,* means to defame.

We see these characteristics everywhere in the world and we might wonder how they can be "put away". Becoming aware of them within ourselves is the real challenge. We have to be strong too as we notice them in our thoughts. Our thoughts are mostly out of control, impressions enter into us and our thoughts wander aimlessly. In this way they control us and yet we must learn to control them. This means that as we become aware of these thoughts we must then replace them with other thoughts. Rudolf Steiner speaks about this as endurance. Rather than being swept away with negative inclinations, through our own initiative - and that is the important part - we remain calm and reach a level of understanding of our own nature.

"What it means to understand any being is nowhere better expressed than in a legend about Christ Jesus, which has been preserved for us not in the Gospels, but in a Persian story. Jesus walked with his disciples overland, and they found a rotting dog on the way. The animal looked ugly. Jesus stopped and glanced admiringly at it, saying, "However, what nice teeth has this animal." Jesus saw the beautiful in the ugly. Strive to see the marvelous everywhere in this way, and then you can see something valuable in everything you see. Be like Christ who admired the beautiful teeth of the dead dog. This leads to great tolerance and to the understanding of anything and any being." (edited) Inner Development by Rudolf Steiner, April 19, 1906

This practice leads us to become impartial, and then we can restrain our judgment and listen to all the ideas expressed around us. We can also become aware of the malice, guile, insincerity, envy, and slander in our own thoughts. For this we need to be calm and objective. When we achieve this we are reborn. As *"newborns"* we *"long for the pure spiritual milk"*. These words are not translated accurately. The word translated as 'spiritual' is *logikos* from *logos* which we explored in 1 Peter 1:23-25

A better translation is: As newborns we desire the pure milk of the word. This new birth speaks to us of the birth of our I Am in our consciousness. As we considered previously, the I Am brings new awareness, and we are able to receive the nourishment of the logos, the word or active idea that lies behind creation. This means that we can then understand the truth that lies behind all creation.

Peter then says, *"that by it you may grow up to salvation"*. Salvation is *soteria*, which means safety, delivered from enemies. These enemies are all those forces that prevent us from being reborn. Yet, if we meet this resistance with inner strength they actually help us to give birth to ourselves. This could be likened to labor pains.

Then we have *"tasted the kindness of the Lord"*. Tasted is *geuomai*, which means to 'try the flavor of' and kindness is *chrestos*, which means fit for use, virtuous, goodness. The word kindness suggests something given to us, whereas virtuous means something we have achieved for ourselves. The virtue and the goodness come when we acknowledge the Lord of our being, the I Am.

Each verse in these letters aids our understanding of the role of the growing connection of the I Am in human life. We must do the work and when there is evidence of this work we will be assisted by all the spiritual beings in the Universe. Unfortunately many people sit back and wait for the spiritual beings to act on their behalf. In fact, we can identify two kinds of human responses. One that denies any existence of spiritual beings; they are those who say that this earth is composed of matter, atoms, and we only live once. The other wafts off into spiritual experiences, denying the reality of the earth, saying that it is maya. These are the two forces working against our rebirth.

These two forces are attractive because we think that we can sit back so that they can do the work. Peter is suggesting that we start with the work of becoming conscious of all the judgmental thoughts that flow through our soul. Painful as this work may be, we will immediately feel supported by that logos power that sustains all creation.

Come to him, to that living stone, rejected by men but in God's sight chosen and precious; and like living stones be yourselves built into a spiritual house, to be a holy priesthood, to offer spiritual sacrifices acceptable to God through Jesus Christ. For it stands in scripture: "Behold, I am laying in Zion a stone, a cornerstone chosen and precious, and he who believes in him will not be put to shame." I Peter 2:4-6

What are we to make of these words? They seem unfathomable. What does it actually mean to be a living stone? How can we become a holy priesthood? And what is an acceptable spiritual sacrifice?

We can only make some sense of this text if we understand and experience the true nature of our being. As physical, etheric, astral and I beings we stand between heaven and earth with a purpose. This purpose is to transform our lower human principle to a higher human principle. This is a process that requires repeated incarnations on this earth.

Understanding reincarnation is the most important task for the whole of humanity. If it is properly understood we will think differently about so many things that take place on the earth. The list is endless but to name a few; the death of children, miscarriages, down syndrome, poverty, natural disasters, sudden accidents and so on. Each of these human experiences contributes to the creation of the higher human principle. We can only see how this happens if we are able to see the many lives each person lives, or, indeed, the many lives that we live on this earth.

Once we begin to understand this to the point where it lives in us, we begin to develop within us the living stone. The living stone is, of course, Christ. His life upon this earth showed us what it meant give life to the physical substance of this earth. This is exactly what his crucifixion and resurrection achieved. He gave new life to this dying earth by infusing it with his being. He made it a living stone. In so doing, he gave us access to the same process.

What happened at the time Jesus lived and participated in this process was that humanity was too attached to the earth. They had lost sight of their true purpose. They didn't see the 'stone' phase as a temporary stage in their many incarnations. Hence they rejected the Christ-ening Jesus because he made them feel unsettled. There would have been a resonating inner voice whispering the truth to them but they rejected it because it disturbed their comfortable life.

"In God's sight" Christ Jesus was *"chosen and precious"*. Precious; *entimos*, means honor, reverence. This is exactly how we must approach all the challenges in our lives, challenges which are our karma - the consequences of our actions in previous lives. Challenges, without which, we cannot transform our lower human principle to a higher human principle.

Our purpose is invigorated when we become living stones. The Greek word 'living' is *zao* which means the spiritualized life-force or I Am infused etheric. This happens when our etheric body becomes more mobile, more energized, and enlivens our physical body. This is turn assists us to read the memory engraved in our etheric body, especially the memory of our previous lives. When we are able to do this from the perspective of our higher human principle, our I Am, we build our spiritual house through our karma.

Then Peter speaks to us about being part of a holy priesthood. In this way he is telling each of us that we will become priests able to offer spiritual sacrifices. Surely this does not mean that we will join a church and train to be ordained. Peter seems to be telling us that when we enliven our etheric bodies and become living (*zao*) stones, we will also become priests. As we connect with our I Am, which is the highest goal of all human beings, we ordain ourselves. This is not a once only event; it is a continual process of ordaining that takes place as we maintain the 'living stone' activity in our being. In this way we are able to offer *"acceptable spiritual sacrifices"*.

What does it mean to offer spiritual sacrifices? Is this what it means to deal with our karma insightfully? Reacting to our karma is the lower human principle. Seeing behind the karma to its cause is the higher human principle. Then we are the priest - first of all to ourselves.

Using these basic principles we can understand the quote Peter uses, *"Behold, I am laying in Zion a stone, a cornerstone chosen and precious, and he who believes in him will not be put to shame."* Zion is the hill on which the higher and more ancient part of Jerusalem was built. Here the corner stone was laid on which we are to build our spiritual house, our higher human principle, our I Am. Our I Am is set within us in a similar way. On it we must build our being, not on the earthly principles, the lower human principles that we are drawn to. Then, as we look at our actions in previous lives, we will not experience shame; we will understand that every action is a stone towards our true life.

To you therefore who believe, he is precious, but for those who do not believe, "The very stone which the builders rejected has become the head of the corner," and "A stone that will make men stumble, a rock that will make them fall"; for they stumble because they disobey the word, as they were destined to do. But you are a chosen race, a royal priesthood, a holy nation, God's own people, that you may declare the wonderful deeds of him who called you out of darkness into his marvelous light. Once you were no people but now you are God's people;

once you had not received mercy but now you have received mercy. I Peter 2:7-10

These words are addressed to those who believe and those who don't. To believe in something is to have confidence in it. In our search for understanding we have to begin with believing. Then we continually test what we believe to be true. This testing process may never end; each new idea must fit into our beliefs like a hand fits into a glove. Those who believe, Peter says, are precious, *time,* the Greek term for "a valuing by which the price is fixed," it is the price we pay for something. What is the price we pay for our belief in Christ Jesus? We set ourselves apart from those who do not believe in him. We can't discuss our belief with them because they will reject what we say. More than that, they will distance themselves from us. How do we deal with this?

If we only mix with those who share our ideas we close ourselves off, but if we keep our ideas to ourselves and mix freely with all those around us, we achieve a much greater purpose. The way we express our beliefs in basic life principles is then an example of the way to approach life.

The example Peter gives is, "The very stone which the builders rejected has become the head of the corner." These words are hard to apply with today's consciousness. If we think of all aspects of the word 'corner' we might be able to apply the idea to our confidence in what we believe. The word corner, *gonia,* means a corner of which there are two aspects; an external angle, or an internal corner, i.e. a secret place.

This whole text is pointing to the continual evolution of human consciousness - an internal secret corner. We each develop our consciousness in our own way, we each move individually from darkness to light. This directs us to the need for mercy, *eleos,* which means showing kindness or goodwill towards others, but also to ourselves. Respecting others for the position of their ideas is essential and as long as we remain open to all possibilities, we continually test our own position. This means that we suspend disagreement; we don't try to draw others towards our way of thinking, but remain open to all ideas always comparing them with our own understanding.

One of the most important things we must do in our daily life is to consider the evolution of consciousness. This is the only way to make sense of all the different ideas we encounter. In the evolution of consciousness, we came from an all-knowing position, we were part of the All, and then, as we individualize, we reached a self-knowing position. We are at the stage now where we are working our way to being a self-knowing part of the all-knowing. In this process, we don't lose our sense of being an individual, and as individuals we work together cooperatively with one purpose. This is our destiny.

Peter's words about people being destined to stumble apply to all of us: *"for they stumble because they disobey the word, as they were destined to do."* When we left our all-knowing position stumbling was the only way to achieve our individuality. Physical rocks and stones inform us of the spiritual challenges we face. In fact, if we interpret everything in the physical world into a spiritual lesson, we will progress more quickly and become chosen.

When Peter speaks about being chosen, we automatically assume that some are chosen and others are rejected. Chosen *eklekto*s, is from the Greek word *eklegomai* which means to pick or choose out for one's self. This does not speak of someone choosing us, but that we do the choosing. Being chosen or rejected is our own call.

Then we come across the strange words, *"Once you were no people but now you are God's people."* What does it mean to be 'no people'? People, in the Greek, is *laos*, which means tribe or nation, in other words, group consciousness. This is backing up the idea of being all-knowing, being part of the greater group. It is through our own choice, our own endeavor, that we become God's people. We become the self-knowing ones who gather together with the Gods who create this Universe, a task which we now assist with as we move towards the greater goal.

Why would we have once not received mercy? Peter is reminding us that through the creation process we moved from not needing mercy to needing it. Mercy, *eleeo,* is kindness or good will towards others. Early in evolution we didn't need mercy because we were guided by the Gods of creation. As we became self-knowing we were able to make mistakes. If these mistakes were made in our attempt to become self-knowing then we received mercy. Of course, those who used the freedom of becoming self-knowing for selfish purposes were excluded from this mercy. On the other hand, if we recognized others who were striving to become self-knowing and through this process made mistakes, we would show them mercy. In this way we began to develop the new community which is our purpose now.

Beloved, I beseech you as aliens and exiles to abstain from the passions of the flesh that wage war against your soul. Maintain good conduct among the Gentiles, so that in case they speak against you as wrongdoers, they may see your good deeds and glorify God on the day of visitation. Be subject for the Lord's sake to every human institution, whether it be to the emperor as supreme, or to governors as sent by him to punish those who do wrong and to praise those who do right. For it is God's will that by doing right you should put to silence the ignorance of foolish men. I Peter 2:11-15

These verses are very overbearing and suggest that we are watched and ruled over by those in positions of power. Perhaps this is the way the translators understood the situation, especially the edicts from the church. Also, perhaps this is the only way the Bible could have been translated at the time so that feathers were not ruffled. Those who had personal insight were left to read between the lines and adjust their behavior accordingly.

Peter calls us aliens and exiles. One of the meanings of 'aliens', *paroikos*, is the one who lives on earth as a stranger. Exiles , *parepidemos* from *par*, which means near, and, *epidemeo*, meaning to be a sojourner, of a foreign resident.

This describes our life on earth. We are beings of soul and spirit who dwell temporarily on this planet. We do this for a purpose, and our task is to work out what this purpose is. As we do this we must become aware of the power of the flesh. Understanding these passions, *epithymia*, which means desire, craving, longing, a desire for what is forbidden or lust, gives us great insight into the relationship between physical and spiritual life. If we look deeply enough we can see that our longing for our spiritual home can be revealed in physical desires. Our task is to create balance and we do this by deeply appreciating the gift of the earth without getting carried away. We see each day as sacred and in this way we enliven our soul rather than wage war, *strateuomai*, meaning fight. If we think about it we will soon identify the elements of this fighting that often takes place within us.

Maintaining good conduct among the Gentiles directs our attention to the need to fit in with the group soul. We don't need to be part of it, but we can understand its place. The inclination is to criticize those who do not live with an understanding of their soul and spirit living in a temporary body. Rather than criticize them we should view them with encouragement for the work they will do. This releases an energy that enables them for the task, whereas criticism imprisons them in their earthly expression. This is what the words "Maintain good conduct" means. Conduct *anastrophe*, means manner of life, conduct, behavior, and comes from the word *anastrepho*, meaning to turn upside down, to change.

It is not difficult to see that if those who develop a spiritual view criticize those who don't the two parties will become estranged. Our task is to avoid this so that *"they may see your good deeds and glorify God on the day of visitation."* The day of visitation is a strange term. Visitation is *episcope*, which means investigation or inspection. This speaks about a time when those who are still developing their experience of soul and spirit while living on the earth will understand those who have already developed this.

Then Peter issues a warning; *"Be subject for the Lord's sake to every human institution,"*. He is not telling us to obey others, which is what the word subject, *hypotasso*, means; to be subordinate, to obey, but rather he is telling us to obey our inner selves. The human institution, *ktisis*, means creation, from *ktizo*, meaning to make habitable, to create, form, shape, transform. This directly refers to our earthly form through which we can do inner work rather than being subject to an external organization.

The emperor and governors are the leaders within our soul. Once we begin to awaken our soul so that our spirit can become active within us, we need to direct this activity in the right way, as any good emperor or governor would. The challenge arises from the anti-forces who work against us. We can see them as a force of resistance which, if met in the right way, will propel us forward. We should also understand that without these forces our development would not be as significant.

Then we *"put to silence the ignorance of foolish men"*. Our first instinct is to think this is about others, yet we are also 'men', *anthropos*. Ignorance, *agnosia*, means not knowing; and foolish, *aphron*, means without reason, indicating the absence of thinking. This is the challenge for every human being who incarnates on this earth: to know and to think.

Rudolf Steiner stressed in many places that we must

experience the permeation of our thought-life by Christ.

"We must consider anew, in a completely factual way, the spiritual-soul content of man, the thought-world which receives into itself the transforming Christ-principle, in order that, through the Christ in us, that is, in our thought-world, we may discover again the spiritual world. Are we to rest content with leaving our thought-world alone at the level to which the Fall of Man has brought it? Shall man's thought-world have no part in human redemption?" Rudolf Steiner, "The Redemption of Thinking" Lecture 3

Live as free men, yet without using your freedom as a pretext for evil; but live as servants of God. Honor all men. Love the brotherhood. Fear God. Honor the emperor. Servants, be submissive to your masters with all respect, not only to the kind and gentle but also to the overbearing. For one is approved if, mindful of God, he endures pain while suffering unjustly. For what credit is it, if when you do wrong and are beaten for it you take it patiently? But if when you do right and suffer for it you take it patiently, you have God's approval. I Peter 2:16-20

Peter advises us to live freely; the word 'men' is not in this text. This freedom is meant in an ethical sense. It doesn't mean to feel free to do whatever we want; it means to be free of personal motives. If we examine our motives carefully we will discover that often when we experience the idea of freedom it is based on an intention to influence others, which is evil, *kakia*, which also means ill-will, desire to injure.

To live as servants, *doulos*, of God does not mean that we surrender ourselves, quite the opposite. *Doulos* means to be devoted to another and to the disregard of one's own interests. These interests are usually the personal motives which we think we are free to express. This involves the activity of our will which we are becoming aware of at this stage of the evolution of our consciousness.

Then we are told to honor, love, and fear. Honor, *timao*, means value; love, *agapao* is the highest love, love without any personal motive; and fear, *phobeo*, means to flee, but it also means to experience awe.

It is important to understand fear because fear is something to be overcome. Mostly we suppress fear as Rudolf Steiner explains.

"A soul investigator may come across the following: In ordinary life the human being finds support and strength by checking the fear that lives in his subconsciousness. But a spiritual investigator cannot fail to see the fear which always lives in the soul's depths. He enters the spiritual world by overcoming this fear. If this fear rises to the surface without entering human consciousness, if it knocks at the door, as it were, and a person ignores it in spite of all, what takes place and what enables that person to overlook this feeling? He pushes down fear, as it were, by denying the existence of the spiritual world." March 9, 1913 How Can We Gain Knowledge of the Supersensible Worlds?

Peter is telling us that we must acquire the strength to bear the sight of the spiritual world. We could refer to the spiritual worlds as God, and in this sense our fear, our awe of the spiritual worlds demands our attention, especially now. In these Seven Letters we are being shown how to do this in many different ways.

Peter then addresses the servants; these are different servants, not *doulos*, but *oiketes*, the one who lives in the same house as another, from *oikeo*, meaning to dwell in. These servants could be all the aspects that dwell in our consciousness and serve our master, our I Am. These aspects must be submissive, *hypotasso; hypo* means by or under, and *tasso* means to put in order. This makes sense of being submissive *"not only to the kind and gentle but also to the overbearing."* Kind, *agathos*, means to be of good constitution or nature; gentle, *epieike*s, means suitable, equitable, or fair. Overbearing, *skolio*s, means crooked or curved and comes from the word *skelos* which means the leg, from the hip to the toes inclusive. This speaks to us of our ability to walk which is directly linked to the forces of our will which we must not impose upon others.

In the next verse some of the translated words don't express what is really meant. *"For one is approved if, mindful of God, he endures pain while suffering unjustly."* The word 'approved' is *charis* which means grace, and the word 'mindful', *syneidesis*, means conscience. It is a prolonged form of *syneido* which means to see together with others, to know another. This perfectly describes the processes within us when we see others from the position of the I Am. We experience each other as if we were them. We enter into each other without influencing the other, with great respect for who they are.

Then we are called upon to think about enduring pain, both if we deserve it, and if we don't. This is directly referring to the life of Jesus who endured much pain that was not deserved. When it says *"For what credit"*, the word credit is *kleos,* meaning either rumor or report, or glory or praise. This speaks of reputation. We must always be conscious of the fact that our spiritual development is continually revealed to everyone through the way we express our feelings, and the way we think and act. This forms our reputation.

Doing wrong, *hamartano,* means to miss the mark, to sin. But if we do right, *agathopoieo,* meaning to do good, to do something which profits others, then we suffer patiently and have *"God's approval."* In other words, our patience is rewarded by God's grace. We might even wonder how we experience this suffering. Suffer, *pascho,* means to have been affected, to feel, have a sensible experience. This can be in a good or bad sense. In fact, the way we experience suffering can indicate whether we meet it with our lower or Higher Self.

For to this you have been called, because Christ also suffered for you, leaving you an example, that you should follow in his steps. He committed no sin; no guile was found on his lips. When he was reviled, he did not revile in return; when he suffered, he did not threaten; but he trusted to him who judges justly. He himself bore our sins in his body on the tree, that we might die to sin and live to righteousness. By his wounds you have been healed. For you were straying like sheep, but have now returned to the Shepherd and Guardian of your souls. I Peter 2:21-25

Peter is explaining that we have been called to suffer, to be affected by earthly events. Often we avoid the experience of being affected yet if we embrace it our experience may surprise us. Suffering experienced by the lower self is self-absorbing; we intensify it by holding it within us. By doing this we sin, *hamartia*, we miss the mark. Holding the suffering in also means we have guile, *dolos*, a word which comes from *deleazo*, which means to bait, catch by a bait. This speaks to us about the way we blame others for our suffering. We bait them in a way that they also suffer which brings us a sense of satisfaction.

This is not what we have been called for. Called, *kaleo*, has several meanings. It means to call aloud, to invite, and it also means to bear a name or title. Being called is at the same time a title, but it is also about being given a name. We each have a cosmic name; we could say that it is the eternal name by which we are known when we stand in our Higher Self. The name we have in this life is a name for that part of us that incarnates time and again, each time the name will probably be different.

A name also indicates our nature, and each incarnation has a different purpose which contributes to changing our nature depending on whether we express our lower or Higher Self. Our eternal name indicates the nature of our Higher Self. When we are called, we are called by our eternal name. We then begin to express the nature of our eternal name in each incarnation. For this reason we don't hit back at others because we know that each experience, as it relates to karma, gives us the opportunity to have a closer relationship to our Higher Self. When we arrive at this point we trust *"him who judges justly."* Judge is *krino*, meaning to separate and examine, and in this way restore balance.

"He himself bore our sins in his body on the tree" is a misinterpretation of what takes place. It should read that we bear our sins like Jesus did; he doesn't bear our sins. The text is saying that those who themselves carry, *anaphero* - which means to lift up one's self - their sins, will live, *zao*, which is our life force, our etheric. In other words, personally bearing our sins gives us life. The body on the tree is *soma*, which includes our etheric and lower astral - all that is physically required to sustain life on this earth. It is *"on the tree"*, it is positioned differently; instead of living on the earth from a purely physical perspective, this body now positions itself in the etheric. Trees, and all plants, are etheric beings.

When this takes place we *"die to sin"*. Die is *apogenomenos*, which means to be removed from, depart, die to anything. We die to our total focus on the physical world as we become aware of the etheric life force within us and around us on the earth.

Then Peter says, *"By his wounds you have been healed."* Wounds, *molops*, means wounds that trickle with blood. Our blood is the vehicle of our I Am, our Higher Self. This speaks to us of the changes that take place in our blood as we integrate our I Am into our physical body and we are healed, *iaomai*, meaning to make whole.

The last verse, 25, speaks directly to our own efforts. *"For you were straying like sheep, but have now returned to the Shepherd and*

Guardian of your souls." Sheep, *probaton*, means any four footed animal, a tame animal accustomed to graze. It comes from the word *probaino*, which means to go forwards, to go on. This is a reference to our astral body which is responsible for the movement of our body. Plants don't move because they don't have an astral body which can certainly stray preventing a connection with our Higher Self.

"the Shepherd and Guardian of your souls." speaks to us of our Guardian Angel which guides and guards us until we reconnect consciously with our I Am. When this happens, our Guardian Angel stands back and we take full responsibility for our spiritual development.

It really is interesting to see what can be revealed with esoteric knowledge. Our instinctive response to a text like this is to believe that the work is being done for us. This, in itself, is a test. If we read these words using some of the above suggestions we prevail over the lower self's inclination to sit back and wait for higher beings to do what we need to do ourselves. However, if we find ways to put in our own effort we will be assisted, firstly by our Guardian Angel before our Higher Self has a strong enough connection. Then, as the Higher Self, the I Am, represented by Jesus, makes the connection, the Christ force within us is activated. This is every human being's purpose on this earth, and conditions on the earth will take place to wake us up to this purpose.

CHAPTER 8
1 PETER 3

Likewise you wives, be submissive to your husbands, so that some, though they do not obey the word, may be won without a word by the behavior of their wives, when they see your reverent and chaste behavior. Let not yours be the outward adorning with braiding of hair, decoration of gold, and wearing of fine clothing, but let it be the hidden person of the heart with the imperishable jewel of a gentle and quiet spirit, which in God's sight is very precious. I Peter 3:1-4

Surely we are not meant to take the first verse literally. We also cannot skip over it thinking that it may have applied when it was written but now that is no longer the case. The following ideas can inspire us to think more deeply about what Peter means.

"Now we must ask: what are the wife and the husband within us?

In a very basic, generalized way we know that the feminine nature is the nurturer, filled with feeling. The male nature is more practical, more pragmatic, based on thinking. Our task is to encourage these two to work together so that feeling warms the coldness of our thinking and thinking guides our feeling to be practical.

Submissive in Greek is hupotasso, where hupo means under, and tasso means to arrange. We can understand that he is saying we arrange our feelings under our thoughts and in this way we keep our emotions under control." Kristina Kaine, The Bible Unlocked

Human development depends on individual human beings controlling their own consciousness. It is not about doing this successfully, it is about putting in the effort. Every attempt strengthens us, and changes us, which sets an example for others to do that same. We don't tell others what to do; we show them other ways to be.

This is indicated by the words about husbands, *"so that some, though they do not obey the word,"* The word is the *logos*, that eternal essence that created the Universe, and indeed continues to create it. The words, *"not obey", apeitheo,* mean not to allow one's self to be persuaded. We live in a time where we resist persuasion. We are committed to our personal thoughts and take a lot of convincing to be influenced by the ideas of others. The only thing that may influence us is observing something different in the behavior of others.

Behavior, *anastrophe,* means manner of life, conduct, and comes from the word *anastrepho,* meaning to turn upside down, overturn, to turn one's self about. This helps us understand that if a wife changes her behavior the husband may take notice. No amount of talking or persuading will change another person but if they see someone change the way they approach life they will be influenced. In this way the change comes about from within each individual which is how it is supposed to be. Then we free ourselves from imposing our ideas on others.

Peter then applies these principles to all of us, not just

married couples. He speaks about the superficial way we can act while within us we have not changed. We hold on to our ideas but outwardly we adorn ourselves with finery. The word adorning is *kosmos*, which means many things in Greek, from an apt and harmonious arrangement or constitution, order, government, to the world, the Universe. It comes from the word *komizo*, meaning to care for, take care of, provide for. Peter is saying that this adorning should not be outward, *"but let it be the hidden person of the heart"*.

Our work is inner work. The challenge is to become aware of our inner consciousness. Do we notice every tiny thought that flashes through our mind when we observe the outer world? Do we judge others secretly and pretend that we didn't have these thoughts? This is adorning ourselves with fine clothes and gold.

Peter is telling us to *"let it be the hidden person of the heart with the imperishable jewel of a gentle and quiet spirit, which in God's sight is very precious."* If we are in God's sight, *enopion*, we are in his presence. How often do we think of ourselves as being in God's presence? If we did we would never think one thing and do another. Perhaps this is why we are not in God's presence very often because we don't measure up. Yet, if we are honest with ourselves, we want to be in God's sight, in his presence. The choice is ours. Can we monitor our thoughts so that they are true in both their inner and outer aspect?

If we manage our thoughts and allow our thoughts to guide our feelings, we enter into that state of eternity. This is that state where we are connected with our eternal being, our I Am. This state is hidden within our hearts; it is not displayed superficially, egotistically. To live this way sets us apart from society and requires strength of character to maintain. At first we can feel that we are not normal, yet we are trying to escape from what is considered normal. We are escaping from the *"braiding of hair, decoration of gold, and wearing of fine clothing"* to the *"imperishable jewel"*. If we hold this image in our hearts it will inspire us to be confident in the face of judgments that can turn us away from the imperishable jewel that is our I Am.

So once the holy women who hoped in God used to adorn themselves and were submissive to their husbands, as Sarah obeyed Abraham, calling him lord. And you are now her children if you do right and let nothing terrify you. Likewise you husbands, live considerately with your wives, bestowing honor on the woman as the weaker sex, since you are joint heirs of the grace of life, in order that your prayers may not be hindered. Finally, all of you, have unity of spirit, sympathy, love of the brethren, a tender heart and a humble mind. I Peter 3:5-8

The second last verse puts everything into perspective by explaining what it means for men and women to be *"joint heirs of the grace of life."* To get to this point we must consider as many aspects as possible of the human expression to be either male or female. We can ask what it means to be male or female but at the same time we should consider that we have been male in some previous lives and female in others. Perhaps we incarnate as a male because we needed to express stronger male qualities, or as a female because we needed to be submissive. There can be very many reasons which only we can personally try to understand.

The basic principles of reincarnation reveal that a person incarnated in a male body will have incarnated in a female body in a previous life, and will do so in a future life. A time will come when we will no longer need to experience being male or female. In fact these two expressions are already beginning to merge; increasingly we see androgynous human beings in society.

We could also interpret these words as advice for

managing the male and female expressions within us. As we have considered, the male expression relates to thinking as the female expression relates to feeling. As a male there can be the challenge of expressing feelings and for females to activate thinking. As we evolve, our thinking, feeling and will become much more controlled and balanced. This depends on our level of awareness as we navigate life and karma. When we reach high levels of awareness we become holy, pure.

When Peter says, *"bestowing honor on the woman as the weaker sex"* the Greek words say woman as the weaker vessel, *skeuos*, not sex. This tells us that women are to be valued for occupying a vessel that is not as strong as the male's vessel. This does not give cause to judge either expression, but rather to respect the soul's choice for incarnating into a male or a female vessel.

Then we get to the point of recognizing that we are *"joint heirs of the grace of life"*. The *"grace of life"* sounds so majestic. It gives us a sense of our destiny. We live with such uncertainty, especially at the moment when the whole of the earth lives under the threat of a virus causing many thousands of people to die. Are we thinking about what it means for the spiritual worlds to be filled with so many souls leaving their bodies, divesting themselves of the distinction of a male or female body? At the same time, it is Easter; the festival of the death of Jesus and resurrection of Christ.

What does it mean to be an heir of the grace of life? We considered the meaning of grace, *charis*, earlier: "Grace is the ability to have full control over all our feelings, thoughts, and actions. It is the ability to see God or the highest in everyone and everything. Then all our responses are graceful." This grace is connected with life, *zoe*, which refers to the spiritualized life-force or I Am infused etheric. When our etheric is infused with our I Am we are in a state of resurrection - which is the purpose of Easter.

Then Peter says, *"Finally, all of you, have unity of spirit, sympathy, love of the brethren, a tender heart and a humble mind."*

We have unity of spirit when we experience the resurrection process, and we are no longer male or female. This is something we can experience in moments during the day when we are able to respond to life through the consciousness of our I Am. This is the true meaning of sympathy, *sympathies*, which means to suffer or feel pain together. We feel the other person's pain as if it were our own, this is the core characteristic of the I Am.

The love of the brethren, *philadelphos*, which means loving brother, is a core experience when we become aware of Christ within us, then we join the brotherhood of Christ. This brotherhood does not depend on race, color, religion, creed, or gender, in fact it embraces these differences.

A tender heart, *eusplanchnos*, means to be compassionate. This is when we overcome the urges of our instinctive astral self-feeling and transform this feeling into forgiveness and understanding. We are able to enter into others and experience their joy or sorrow as we would experience our own.

Finally, we have a humble mind, *philophron*, the mind-set of love which is quick to show friendly, courteous behavior.

Bringing our awareness to the ways in which we respond to life for each of these points brings us closer to experiencing the reality of the resurrected Christ in each one of us. Even saying to ourselves "Christ is in you" to each person that comes to our attention will assist us to experience the truth of the Easter process.

Do not return evil for evil or reviling for reviling; but on the contrary bless, for to this you have been called, that you may obtain a blessing. For "He that would love

life and see good days, let him keep his tongue from evil and his lips from speaking guile; let him turn away from evil and do right; let him seek peace and pursue it. For the eyes of the Lord are upon the righteous, and his ears are open to their prayer. But the face of the Lord is against those that do evil." I Peter 3:9-12

Understanding evil is an important task for us, especially at this stage of our evolution. On our evolutionary journey we are becoming more spiritualized which requires us to fully understand the difference between the material world and the spiritual worlds. What takes place in the spiritual worlds cannot be expressed on the earth, and some things can only be developed on the earth, others only in spirit. We have the freedom to work this out.

Evil is the testing ground for our freedom. Peter says, "Do not return evil for evil" and the word for return in the Greek is *apodidomi*, which also means 'to deliver'. Returning evil for evil gives us a sense of something personal taking place person to person, whereas delivering has a broader sense of distributing beyond the one to one connection. This would suggest that our response affects the Universe.

We should also consider that when someone inflicts something on us, our focus is on them when in fact they could just be the instrument so that we experience something that could have little to do with them. This is the way karma works. Each of us must meet circumstances in life that assists us to compensate for our actions in a past life. In this way each of us is given the opportunity to claim our own freedom. We can decide how to respond to the situation: with a blessing or a curse.

Whenever we deal with difficulties in life we should be aware that some people are able to step up as the force of opposition, not because they were the victim of our actions in a past life but because they are called to give us the opportunity to express our freedom. Yet, most of the time, we blame the person who presents the difficulty. This also means that we engage with the difficulty giving up our opportunity to be free.

We must strive to understand that it is our purpose to become free beings. To be free is a very powerful position in the universe. This freedom is earned as we go through many tests. Rudolf Steiner speaks of evil and freedom in many different ways in his lectures. On the 13th February 1917 he was speaking about the development of human consciousness by describing that in the beginning we didn't have only the states of sleeping, dreaming, and waking, but we could also see true spiritual reality. He then said,

"Now, as we know, in order that man should develop the full earth-consciousness, this method of perception had to be withdrawn. If it had persisted, man would never have gained his freedom, he could not have become free if he had not been subjected to all the dangers, arguments and temptations of materialism; but he has to find his way back again to the spiritual world, and must now be able to grasp it in full earth consciousness." Rudolf Steiner "Cosmic and Human Metamorphoses" Lecture 2, The Metamorphoses of the Soul-Forces

To become more conscious is such an important task and The Seven Letters give us very direct guidance in how it can be achieved. When Peter tells us to refrain from responding to evil with evil, he then says that we have been called to "obtain blessing", the word obtain is *kleronomeo*, which means inherit, to be an heir. This suggests that it is through experiencing evil or identifying evil, that we will receive our inheritance, and we have been called to do this.

Then Peter quotes Psalm 35 which suggests that we should behave ourselves because we are being watched by the Lord. If we accept that the Bible tells us of the human journey from being an indivisible part of the whole universe to becoming an individual, then we can also understand that the Old Testament predicts the Christ event which we read about in the New Testament. The purpose of the Christ event was to give us a direct connection with our I Am, and this I Am can be interpreted as the Lord. When we read the Bible and replace the word 'Lord' with the words 'I Am' we can see a new perspective.

Then our prayer, *deesis*, which means need, what is lacking, becomes a conversation between our lower self and our Higher Self. This is not begging some unknown spiritual being to act on our behalf; this is a conversation where we admit to what is lacking in our life as a means of understanding the purpose of the deficiency. It can be something as simple as realizing in the moment that an interaction with others assists us to become more conscious of our I Am. The more we can do this the more it will become a normal part of our consciousness. Then we will never blame others for our difficulties but rather see them as opportunities to see the "face of the Lord", the appearance of our I Am.

PS An excellent lecture on Evil, "Evil in the Light of Spiritual Knowledge" translated by Mark Willan, is available on the Steiner Archive rsarchive.org

Now who is there to harm you if you are zealous for what is right? But even if you do suffer for righteousness' sake, you will be blessed. Have no fear of them, nor be troubled, but in your hearts reverence Christ as Lord. Always be prepared to make a defense to any one who calls you to account for the hope that is in you, yet do it with gentleness and reverence; and keep your conscience clear, so that, when you are abused, those who revile your good behavior in Christ may be put to shame. For it is better to suffer for doing right, if that should be God's will, than for doing wrong. I Peter 3:13-17

These words could describe the life of Jesus, he was harmed, *kakoo*, which means to oppress, and comes from the word, *kakos,* evil, also meaning destructive. Nothing deterred him however. He went about his mission by finding those people who could see a glimmer of truth in all that he revealed.

By reading about the life of Jesus in the Bible we can identify many examples in our own lives, especially when we identify with the importance of the two beings, Jesus and Christ. When these beings take hold of us we do become zealous, *zelotes*, which means to burn with zeal. This doesn't mean that we should use our zeal to convert others; all we need to do is be an example of this zeal in our own lives. This enthusiasm can take on many forms in our lives and it may have no religious context at all. It could be the way we do our job, or manage our relationships, or even just the way we live in small moments of our lives.

One way to exemplify this is not to react to difficulties. Even if we do suffer, *pascho*, which means to be affected - which can be good or bad - we remain composed. This composure is not about hiding what we are feeling; it is about balancing our feelings with our thinking and will in our soul. It is only when we have this soul balance that our spirit can enter into our soul. This is why it cannot be a façade; it has to be a genuine soul experience. Covering up what we are really feeling will always repel our spirit.

So why would we *"suffer for righteousness' sake"*? Righteousness, *dikaiosune,* means justice which involves a series of adjustments in our ideas so that they reach a balance; they don't lean one way or the other. We have to make these adjustments to accommodate our spirit in our soul. Our spirit has a level of purity that challenges our soul's habitual bias. The adjustments are necessary, which is where suffering comes in, so that our soul and spirit can work together.

Suffering, *pascho,* also means passion and points to that inner fire of zealousness that inspires us to do the necessary work. Holding that passion within us rather than expressing it provides us with the energy we need to do the task. Then we will be blessed, *makarios,* which means to be well off, fortunate.

As we go through this process of our spirit-soul infusion we should always remind ourselves of the presence of Christ. The *"fear and trouble"* comes from within us; it does not come from others. Others may question us about our resilient nature; they may even challenge us because we are not acting as they might expect us to. Our defense, *apologia,* which means reason, for the hope, *elpis,* expectation, that is within us, is grounded in meekness - gentleness, and fear (not reverence). Fear is an important human experience; it is through fear that we incarnate, because through fear we experience self-containment, a feeling of self. Again, fear is something that should be held within us as a form of energy.

Keeping our conscience clear is an importance task. Conscience, *syneidesis,* in the Greek means the consciousness of anything, which tells us that we have conscience when we are conscious, not unconscious. Conscience is a faculty, an organ of cognition, which perceives Christ. That would fit with what Peter is saying here.

Then Peter alerts us to the possibility of being abused and reviled. Abused is *katalaleo,* with means to speak against, to defame, and revile, *epereazo,* means to insult or threaten. We must become increasingly aware that when we are able to express our spirit through our soul others can become fearful of us. The psychology of this is a deep matter and if we can't fully understand it we can at least be aware of it so that we don't react when we see the fearful response. It seems a shame that those who behave in this way are *"put to shame."* Perhaps it is better to think that they will experience shame when they are able to observe their behavior at some future time - perhaps after they die and review the life they have just lived.

As we go through the changes necessary for our spiritual development we will always have choices, this is what it means to be an individual, no longer guided by the spiritual worlds and its beings. God's will is not imposed upon us, it is up to us to understand the will of God and align our activity with it. If we don't we can choose evil over good. This is our purpose and our task, to understand the will of God and align ourselves with it.

For Christ also died for sins once for all, the righteous for the unrighteous, that he might bring us to God, being put to death in the flesh but made alive in the spirit; in which he went and preached to the spirits in prison, who formerly did not obey, when God's patience waited in the days of Noah, during the building of the ark, in which a few, that is, eight persons, were saved through water. Baptism, which corresponds to this, now saves you, not as a removal of dirt from the body but as an appeal to God for a clear conscience, through the resurrection of Jesus Christ, who has gone into heaven and is at the right hand of God, with angels, authorities, and powers subject to him. I Peter 3:18-22

Peter now sums up all that he has been saying in chapter 3, and in fact, he sums up the purpose of the life of Jesus the Christen-ed one. He also summarizes our purpose as we work towards spiritualizing ourselves through our many journeys to earth.

Peter uses some of the most misused and misunderstood words in the Bible, words that can only be understood through esoteric knowledge. When he says, *"Christ also died for sins once for all"* this does not mean sins are eliminated, it means that we now have the ability to choose not to sin. Sin, *hamartia*, means missing the mark, missing the bullseye, and we can't hit the bullseye when we can't see the spiritual reality in which we live.

He follows this with the words *"the righteous for the unrighteous"*. We can presume he is saying that Christ is righteous and we are unrighteous which seems quite harsh. The word righteous, *dikaios*, means justice, meaning the ability to know right from wrong, of recognizing justice, and of restoring the balance. Until we can see spiritually we can't fully know right from wrong. Sometimes what we think is right is actually wrong which is how we miss the bullseye.

When we read the words *"being put to death in the flesh but made alive in the spirit,"* we immediately think of the crucifixion of Jesus, yet this is an inner process that we personally go through. The flesh, *sarx*, as was explored previously is *"not our physical body but refers to our astral, our sentient body, that part of us that perceives the things outside us making us aware that we are individuals. The best way to understand this is to think of what happens when we fall asleep; we lose consciousness of the world around us because our astral body leaves our physical (and etheric) body lying there."* James 5:1-3

This tells us that we experience death in our soul so that we can be made alive in our spirit. Made alive, *zoopoieo*, comes from *zoon*, a living being, and can also mean animals, and *poieo*, means to bring into existence. This speaks to us of our earthly manifestation, as spiritual beings we took on the flesh, *sarx*, which we have in common with animals who are astral beings. This is supported by the mention of Noah who took all kinds of animals into the ark to save them from the flood.

The story of Noah and the ark is deeply esoteric. Rudolf Steiner has this to say, *"Before the time of our present humanity there was a kind of water or sea-life that was lived in vessels, in which humanity gradually accustomed itself to life on land. The life of the Atlanteans was for the most part a life in vessels. Not only were they surrounded by a watery, misty air, but a large part of Atlantis was covered by the sea. This is the deep mystery of Noah's Ark."* Occult Signs and Symbols, Lecture 2.

Peter's words contain much esoteric and occult knowledge which we will only understand when we become more spiritually conscious. We should not feel frustrated when we don't fully understand it; we should consider it as a seed which will germinate in the future.

"Preaching to the spirits in prison" is about Christ's journey after the crucifixion into the center of the earth to rescue those beings who had sinned so seriously that they were trapped there. Preach, *kerysso*, is not so much preaching but to proclaim or announce.

It is interesting to consider that the baptism is now *"an appeal to God for a clear conscience"*. Conscience is a faculty we develop as our I Am begins to work consciously in our soul. Sergei Prokofieff explained that conscience is an organ of cognition which perceives Christ.

Then Peter takes us into the heavenly realms and the state of resurrection which we will all experience through our perception of Christ. He points to the spiritual beings who work with us as we experience the spiritual baptism: the angels, authorities, and powers.

The angels, *angelos*, are the messengers, they are one level above us and are the ones who assist us to make sense of the spiritual worlds. Authorities, or *Exousiai* or *Elohim*, are three levels above the Angels and they implanted the 'I' in us in this earth cycle. *"Jehovah is one of the seven Elohim. They are spirits of light and love. Six live on the sun and shine down love in the sunlight, but Jehovah chose the moon to his abode and pours ripened wisdom down upon the earth thus preparing the way for love."* Edited words of Rudolf Steiner, The Gospel of St John.

The powers, *dynamis*, are the spirits of movement, they brought the cosmos into movement. When it says these beings are subject to Christ, the word subject is *hypotasso*, from *hypo*, meaning by or under, and *tasso*, meaning to put in a certain order, to arrange. So these beings are arranged under Christ rather than under his control. By giving deep consideration to these ideas we will increasingly awaken to the presence of Christ with us.

CHAPTER 9
I PETER 4

Since therefore Christ suffered in the flesh, arm yourselves with the same thought, for whoever has suffered in the flesh has ceased from sin, so as to live for the rest of the time in the flesh no longer by human passions but by the will of God. Let the time that is past suffice for doing what the Gentiles like to do, living in licentiousness, passions, drunkenness, revels, carousing, and lawless idolatry. They are surprised that you do not now join them in the same wild profligacy, and they abuse you; but they will give account to him who is ready to judge the living and the dead. I Peter 4:1-4

To understand what Peter is now explaining we need to know what suffering in the flesh really means. Flesh, *sarx*, is that part of our soul that is connected to this physical world while we live in a physical body. We can refer to this as our astral body, it is our sensuous nature, and can be compared to the animal nature of the human being. It is important to understand these aspects of our being otherwise we cannot think through all our different functions.

Our astral body in its natural state can be called the lowest region of our soul. This is where our emotions lie and it is also where our instincts arise. The astral body is also responsible for the movement of the physical body. So we can say that much of what takes place in our astral body is unconscious until we engage with it and become conscious of its activity. As we become more conscious of the activity of the astral body, and as we refine its activity, we become consciously aware of our greater soul where thinking and willing are added to our feeling levels.

While we can say that we are beings of body, soul, and spirit, we can also say that we have a physical body, an etheric body, an astral body, and an I-being. In this sense, physical and etheric are the physical manifestation, the astral is our soul, and our I-being is our spirit. So we can say that *sarx*, our astral body, is also our soul body which, through our own efforts, we refine from an instinctive state to a state of conscious awareness through engagement with our I Am. These are the principles we need to identify in our daily life if we are to understand our true nature.

Understanding that the soul is the focus of our activity when we incarnate into a physical body is important, it is that part of us that has a sentient experience of the physical world. We can't fully understand this if we identify ourselves as simply a physical body. Only when we experience ourselves as a soul which has created a physical body, enabling it to interact with the physical world physically, can we understand this text.

Only when we begin to experience the difference between our body and our soul will we fully understand these words, *"for whoever has suffered in the flesh has ceased from sin"*. This is about being aware of our astral instincts and changing them, directing them in a higher, more conscious way. Becoming aware of these instincts is painful, but until this happens human beings live like the Gentiles. Their responses to life are unconscious guided by instincts that give them pleasure, having no regard for the effect of their behavior on others.

Those who live like Gentiles think they are free to do what they like but they have no idea of true freedom. Rudolf Steiner spoke about it very clearly in a lecture in 1920 when he said, *"there will be freedom in our actions and love in our thinking."* When we achieve this we will, as Peter says, *"live for the rest of the time in the flesh no longer by human passions but by the will of God."*

This is how Rudolf Steiner explains how we achieve freedom and love.

"And because, as man, we are a unified whole, when we reach the point where we find freedom in the life of thought and love in the life of will, there will be freedom in our actions and love in our thinking. Each irradiates the other: action filled with thought is wrought in love; thinking that is permeated with will gives rise to actions and deeds that are truly free.

Thus you see how in the human being the two great ideals, freedom and love, grow together. Freedom and love are also that which man, standing in the world, can bring to realization in himself in such a way that, through him, the one unites with the other for the good of the world." Rudolf Steiner, The Path to Freedom and Love and their Significance in World Events, December 19, 1920

If we can achieve this Peter tells us that we will receive abuse, *blasphemeo*, meaning reproach, from those who have not become conscious of the activity of their soul and spirit. This is why we need to experience true freedom and the highest love. Then we do not feel bound by any abuse coming from others, who are actually just trying to feel better about themselves, and we can love them because we see their struggles. If we are able to respond in this way to those who try to reproach us, we have a chance of demonstrating the benefits of expressing the higher soul levels in the hope of silently influencing their behavior - in this life or the next.

For this is why the gospel was preached even to the dead, that though judged in the flesh like men, they might live in the spirit like God. The end of all things is at hand; therefore keep sane and sober for your prayers. Above all hold unfailing your love for one another, since love covers a multitude of sins. Practice hospitality ungrudgingly to one another. I Peter 4:6-9

A true understanding of the human spirit challenges our understanding of the phrase *"preached even to the dead"*. Are the dead those who have passed through life and have now left their physical bodies? Or does the word dead, *nekros*, meaning without life, speak of those still living on this earth but with no life, no spiritual life within them? Are they so bound to physical life that they have divorced themselves from their soul and spirit? It is important that we experience our soul and spirit as we live our life on this earth, even in simple ways throughout the day. When we enjoy something is it because we are physically satisfied, or is it because we experienced the spiritual gift. To be physically satisfied points to the flesh, *sarx*, the astral element within us which is compared to animal life.

The words *"they might live in the spirit like God"* might be better interpreted as "live according to God's spirit". This is our purpose, to discover God's spirit and to work towards aligning ourselves with it. This is the reason why Christ entered the flesh, died in a physical body, and experienced the resurrection. We can use these three steps in our experience of life on this earth. Then we see the physical for what it is, and then die to it so that we experience the spirit of it. If we can do this more often we will have a greater appreciation for the spirit that underlies all things and in that way live according to God's spirit.

How often do we look at things from Christ's perspective? He lived according to God's spirit. He knew that God, *theos*, encompassed all the deities or divinities guiding the universe, all the higher beings in the Cosmos from Angels to Seraphim who keep everything in balance. This points to the meaning of *"judged in the flesh"*. To judge, *krino*, is that process of separating out all the elements and joining them back together in the right order. If we don't factor in all these elements our judging is limited.

We should also understand that our consciousness is not at the stage where we can put everything in the right order yet. The Gods give us every opportunity to do it, but they are always standing by to assist once we have committed ourselves to work with them.

When Peter says, *"The end of all things is at hand"* he is not speaking of the end of the world. He is speaking about a change in consciousness. The word end, *telos*, means termination, the limit at which a thing ceases to be. It is the end of some act or state, but not of the end of a period of time. The term, *"at hand"* is *engizo* meaning to bring near, to join one thing to another. This is exactly what we are doing now; we are joining our consciousness, developed over thousands of years, to a new level resulting from the Deed of Christ. Again, do we look at this from Christ's perspective?

This Cosmic being is within us, within this earth, and surrounding this earth - all this is his body. He is experiencing us from every perspective. When we think of him in the right way we light up and he responds with his own light. He enhances the light we have created and gives us the opportunity to understand this stage in evolution that we are participating in. Christ wants nothing more than for us to know him and to be conscious of our relationship with him. He does not force this on us; we are at liberty to engage with him as we can. Perhaps this is why Peter says *"keep sane and sober for your prayers"*

Sane and sober in the Greek have a similar meaning. Sane, *sophroneo*, means to be of sound mind, to be in one's right mind, to exercise self-control, to put a moderate estimate upon one's self, to curb one's passions. Sober, *nepho*, means to be sober, to be calm and collected in spirit, to be temperate, dispassionate. Both of these speak to our astral which we work to refine from its instinctive animal levels to higher human levels. We do this with our prayer, *proseuche*, a place set apart or suited for the offering of prayer.

At the heart of all this activity is love, *agape*. Love brings balance to our sins, *hamartia*, the way we miss the mark. Love corrects our aim continually. Then we can *"practice hospitality"*, *philoxenos*, from *philos*, meaning friend or brotherly love, and *xenos*, a foreigner, a stranger. Hospitality means that we are generous to guests and we do this ungrudgingly, *gongysmos*, which means a murmur, muttering, secret debate, to confer secretly. How often are we nice to people while secretly criticizing them?

All of this points to becoming much more aware of our inner soul activity which can be drawn down to the astral level instead of upwards to the consciousness of our I Am.

As each has received a gift, employ it for one another, as good stewards of God's varied grace: whoever speaks, as one who utters oracles of God; whoever renders service, as one who renders it by the strength which God supplies; in order that in everything God may be glorified through Jesus Christ. To him belong glory and dominion for ever and ever. Amen. I Peter 4:10-11

How do we know if we have received a gift? First we must be aware of the gift and then we only experience the gift if we actually take it. The word received is *lambano*, which means to take with the hand, to carry away. Once we have taken the gift, we must then *"employ it for one another"*. The word employ is *diakoneo* which means to minister, to serve. If we really understand this we realize that there can be no ego involved. So often we receive gifts and give gifts for personal satisfaction; we can test this out during our interaction with others throughout the day. It can be as simple as a thank-you. Observe the expectation to be thanked within ourselves and in others.

When we free ourselves from the pull of the ego, we become good stewards. Stewards, *oikonomos,* are the managers of the household, especially the economy of the household. This speaks of the flow of energy, incoming and outgoing. When we are good stewards by serving each other, the flow of energy in and out contains no desire for personal gain.

If this energy is free flowing, when no one seeks the advantage, then we are *"stewards of God's varied grace"*. Varied, *poikilosm*, means various colors, and grace, *charis*, means good will, loving kindness. A deeper meaning of *charis* is the generation of abundance out of nothing. This requires the ability to have full control over all our feelings, thoughts, and actions. This is achieved when we control our ego.

Rudolf Steiner says, *"the soul's capacity for doing right out of the inner self was called Grace. Grace and an inner recognition of truth came into being through the Christ."* Gospel of St John Lecture 4

Peter tells us that when we receive this gift consciously it can be spoken or rendered as a service. Our ability to speak, *laleo*, comes from the human I Am, and we give service, *diakoneo*, (see above) without ego when we act through our I Am. We do this through the strength which God supplies. Strength, *diakoneo*, is ability, a force, and if it is supplied by God we can assume that it is stronger than our own or supplements our own.

The word 'supplies' is interesting. It is the Greek word *choregeo* which means to be a chorus leader, to furnish the chorus at one's own expense, to procure and supply all things necessary to fit out a chorus. This describes the word supply, but it is more than that. A chorus, as the part of a song repeated after each verse, speaks of co-operation, of working together for an outcome. This describes the cooperation between God and those of us who have a consciousness awareness of their I Am.

This happens *"in order that in everything God may be glorified through Jesus Christ"*. Glorified is *doxa*, which means shining like a star. This is the transformed astral, the astral which works with the I Am instead of the ego; this I Am which was given to us by the deed of Christ Jesus. Again we get a sense of the chorus, the joining together to create something that is beyond the ability of one entity. How often do we feel that we bear the weight of our spiritual development alone? Peter is telling us that we are part of a mighty team from which we shine beyond our imaginings. Then we can say Amen.

Valentin Tomberg, in his study of The Revelation, has this to say about the word Amen.

Conscience, in this sense, results from inwardizing experience throughout many incarnations of the soul's past. It is the great moral and spiritual synthesis of all the experiences and revelations which the soul has received. Such comprehensive vision from within outwards was - during the age in which Christianity began - denoted by the word Amen which is now interpreted as meaning "It is certainly true."

He is saying that Amen is the acknowledgement that something hidden in our own inner nature has been revealed which we recognize as true (through what is spoken) - a resurrection from our I.

The resurrection of our I, our sense of self, is the I Am. We received the possibility of experiencing this I Am through the crucifixion and resurrection of Christ. This is what the Seven Letters explain to us. James, Peter, John, and Jude have experienced the resurrected presence of Christ and the emergence of the personal I Am experience, and they want to prepare us for the consequent change. The change will be with us for ever and ever, for eternity. There is no going back. The change, as we know, is not straightforward, and as Peter explains, we can't do it alone. However, he assures us that we are accompanied and supported by God who is glorified through Jesus Christ.

> *Beloved, do not be surprised at the fiery ordeal which comes upon you to prove you, as though something strange were happening to you. But rejoice in so far as you share Christ's sufferings, that you may also rejoice and be glad when his glory is revealed. If you are reproached for the name of Christ, you are blessed, because the spirit of glory and of God rests upon you. I Peter 4:12-14*

Peter is addressing a specific group of people, the beloved. To be addressed as beloved, *agapetos*, means to be part of a special brotherhood (regardless of gender). We belong to this brotherhood if we continually strive to develop spiritually. It is important to understand that striving for spiritual development rather than achieving it is the true task. Often, those who think they have achieved spiritual development stop striving for it.

Then Peter advises those who are part of this brotherhood that a *"fiery ordeal"* will surprise them. The word surprised, *xenizo*, has several meanings. It means to receive as a guest, to be received hospitably, or to stay as a guest, to lodge. It also means to surprise or astonish by the strangeness and novelty of a thing, to be shocked.

The *"fiery ordeal"* in the Greek is *pyrosis* which means a burning. It comes from the word *pyroo* which means to burn with fire and can mean melted by fire and purged of dross. This speaks of the movement of the energy located at the base of the spine called Kundalini fire. Rudolf Steiner explains in this way.

"The Kundalini fire is a force which to-day still slumbers in man, but which will gradually gain more and more importance. To-day it already has a great importance, it has a great influence upon what we perceive through the sense of hearing. During the further development in the sixth sub-race of the fifth root-race [we are presently in the fifth sub-race of the fifth root race] *the Kundalini fire will acquire great influence on what lives in the human heart. The human heart will really have this fire. At first this seems to be mere symbolism but man will then really be permeated by a force which will live in his heart, so that during the sixth root-race he will no longer make a distinction between his own well-being and the well-being of the whole. So deeply will man be permeated by the Kundalini fire! He will follow the principle of love as his own innermost nature."* Rudolf Steiner 28.10.1904

The words in Peter's text which he uses to describe this development within those who belong to the brotherhood support the idea that he speaks of the movement within us of the Kundalini. His words are *"the fiery ordeal which comes upon you"* and the word 'comes' is *ginomai*, which means to become, to be made, to arise, which supports the idea of the rising movement within us of the Kundalini.

Then he says that this fiery ordeal *"comes to prove us"*. The word prove, *peirasmos,* means an experiment, a trial or test and comes from *peirazo* which means to try whether a thing can be done. It also means to make trial of, to test: for the purpose of ascertaining a person's quantity, or what they think, or how they will behave. This explains that our spiritual development is continually tested and the meaning of the Greek word suggests that we do our own testing. Furthermore, It is not once and for all, but ongoing.

Then we have the unusual statement *"as though something strange were happening to you."* This would back up the idea of the Kundalini. The word strange is not in the Greek, it just says 'thing happened'. Thing in Greek is *xenos* which means a foreigner, a stranger, an alien, something new, unheard of.

Happened is *symbaino* which means to walk with the feet near together, to come together, or of things which fall out at the same time, to happen, come to pass. *Symbaino* comes from *syn*, meaning with, and *basis*, meaning a stepping, walking, foot. If we take all these meanings into consideration we can see that the word is certainly speaking of a change within us. We have our ability to walk because of our I Am and as we integrate our I Am into our being we experience it as a stranger. As our I Am moves through our being it activates our spiritual centers (chakras) through the movement of the Kundalini fire and we are changed.

Then we rejoice! Rejoice is *agalliao*, which means to exult, be exceeding glad, and comes from *agan* (much) and *hallomai*, meaning to leap, to spring up, gush up; of water. This gushing up again speaks to us of the rising of the Kundalini from the base of the spine.

The rejoicing comes from sharing Christ's sufferings which indicates that through our spiritual development we see the truth. When the truth reveals to us how much is misunderstood it is very painful. Peter tells us that at the same time Christ's glory is revealed. His glory, *doxa*, is the shining of his purified astral which is revealed to us. The Greek word for revealed is *apokalypsis*, meaning to lay bare, make naked, a disclosure of truth, instruction concerning things before unknown.

The Peter says, *"If you are reproached for the name of Christ, you are blessed,"*. Does this mean that to be reproached is the sign of the presence of Christ within us? Will we only know we have progressed in our spiritual development when we are reproached? Then we will know that we are blessed because the spirit of glory (*doxa*) and of God rests upon us.

But let none of you suffer as a murderer, or a thief, or a wrongdoer, or a mischief-maker; yet if one suffers as a

Christian, let him not be ashamed, but under that name let him glorify God. For the time has come for judgment to begin with the household of God; and if it begins with us, what will be the end of those who do not obey the gospel of God? And "If the righteous man is scarcely saved, where will the impious and sinner appear?" Therefore let those who suffer according to God's will do right and entrust their souls to a faithful Creator. I Peter 4:15-19

We might wonder why Peter gives a list of the types of 'sins' we could commit, *"a murderer, or a thief, or a wrongdoer, or a mischief-maker"*. Why these and not others? Why do these cause suffering? It is always helpful to ask questions because it leads us closer to the true meaning of what is being said. The word suffer, *pascho*, can be good or bad. It means to be affected, to feel, to experience. When suffering is a painful experience it indicates that our ego is involved. If we can experience it in a higher way it means that our I Am is active in our soul.

When we reach this stage of development we then become aware of the ways in which we murder others through our thoughts, feelings, and actions. Then we see the satisfaction we experienced by taking the life out of others. Then we truly suffer, but in a good way. Rudolf Steiner spoke of this in 1921, *"Enclosed within him (man) he has a fiery center of destruction, and in truth the forces of decline can be transformed into forces of ascent only if he becomes conscious of this fact."* 23 September, 1921

When we experience suffering in a transformative way, as Christ Jesus did during the crucifixion, we glorify God. We transform the lower astral impulses that draw us towards the forces of decline and we become Christian, *Christiano*s, Christened. This rests on our ability to become conscious of why we suffer, of the way we are a murderer, *phoneus*, from *phonos*, to murder or slaughter; or a thief, *kleptes*, from *klepto*, to steal, take away by theft or stealth. Can we identify all the ways we steal from others each day? It could be as simple as their ideas. Peter continues his list by saying that we can also be a wrongdoer, *kakopoios*, which means to be an evil doer, a producer of evil. As we have previously considered, evil is necessary but only if we are conscious of it. It is the force of resistance that makes it possible for us to take flight. Peter's fourth impulse is the mischief-maker, *allotriepiskopos*, which means a meddler in the affairs of others. How often do you engage in this?

Then we are told not to be ashamed, *aischynomai*, which means to disfigure, to dishonor, to suffuse with shame, *"but under that name let him glorify God."* The literal translation of verse 16 says this: If yet as a Christian not ashamed, glorify moreover this god with this name, this one's true self *(houtos)*.

What is *"that name"*? That name is the only name we are known by in the universe, "I Am". This reinforces the idea that it is only when we can view the cause of suffering within us from the point of view of the I Am will we be able to bear the destructive forces within us. When we achieve this we glorify God.

By experiencing our name, I Am, our true self, and identifying these impulses within us, then we are in step with Peter's words, *'For the time has come for judgment to begin with the household of God;'*. The household of God is within us and the judgment is a positive process of weighing everything up and balancing it out. Judgment, *krima*, comes from the word *krino* which means to separate. We separate all the individual facts and put them together in accordance with God's original ideas. At the core of his ideas we find the idea of the human being, the one destined to become a god through the I Am. This idea is explained by St John in his Gospel in many different ways, especially through the seven I Am statements.

Peter then puts forward some disturbing ideas for us to contemplate. *'If* (this process) *begins with us'*: begins, *proton*, first in time or place; us, *ego*, *"what will be the end"* for those who don't begin? The word 'end' is interesting, as we have previously noted. It is the last in any succession or series, so it is not the final end. This should tell us that there is always hope. Those who *"do not obey"*, *apeitheo*, which means do not allow themselves to be persuaded, or refuse or withhold belief, always have a chance to change. This is the way we should look upon all those who do not share our insight.

Then Peter says, *"If the righteous man is scarcely saved, where will the impious and sinner appear?"* The righteous, *dikaios*, are those who make adjustments but who are then scarcely saved; scarcely, *molis*, means with difficulty, not easily. It is always helpful to remember that our task involves effort and the effort is rewarded, not the result. Will, *thelema*, means to have in mind, to be determined. Peter is reminding us that our spiritual development involves commitment and effort and that we shouldn't judge those who are not able to make this commitment at the moment. If they see that some people can do it then perhaps in their next life they will do it to.

CHAPTER 10
I PETER 5

So I exhort the elders among you, as a fellow elder and a witness of the sufferings of Christ as well as a partaker in the glory that is to be revealed. Tend the flock of God that is your charge, not by constraint but willingly, not for shameful gain but eagerly, not as domineering over those in your charge but being examples to the flock. And when the chief Shepherd is manifested you will obtain the unfading crown of glory. I Peter 5:1-4

These words explain that no one must rule over others anymore. Previously, a group had a leader who made all the decisions, now each person has the responsibility of leading themselves. This is what the Christ event is all about; it gave people the ability to make their own decisions. This was possible through the implanting of the 'link' to the I Am.

Peter is explaining that people could only begin to

understand what this means if they witnessed Christ's sufferings. Suffering is *pathema* from the Greek word *pathos*, which means whatever befalls one, in other words, destiny. We cannot understand destiny without knowing that we live successive lives on this earth. Destiny is karma. Rudolf Steiner has this to say about destiny and karma.

"Thus man indeed creates his destiny for himself. This remains incomprehensible only as long as one considers the separate life as such and does not regard it as a link in the chain of successive lives. Thus we may say that nothing can happen to the human being in life for which he has not himself created the conditions. Only through insight into the law of destiny — karma — does it become comprehensible why "the good man has often to suffer, while the evil one may experience happiness." How Karma Works GA 34

If we apply these ideas to our daily life we can see how easy it is to misjudge people. If we become the true witness, *martys*, the one who experiences what others experience as if it was happening to them, we become the elder. Elders, *presbyteros*, essentially mean those who have the most experience. Our task is to become elders by having firsthand experiences of the Christ event. Not simply seeing him nailed to a cross and killed by the leaders at that time, but as the one who brought to us the I Am which gives us the ability to lead ourselves. We do this by contemplating all the details this involved and identifying them in our own lives, particularly in our consciousness.

When we read words like *"Tend the flock of God that is your charge"* we can understand why many people take on leadership roles and tell others what to do. Charge, *episkopeo*, means to observe, to contemplate. Peter is quite clear that this means to be an example. This does not just mean in actions, but in thoughts and feelings as well. When we take up the task of being aware of every thought and feeling we can be alarmed by the negativity and judgment in our consciousness.

The Chief Shepherd is Christ, and when he is manifested in us we will *"obtain the unfading crown of glory"*. Unfading, *amarantinos*, means composed of amaranth, a flower so called because it never withers or fades, and when picked, revives if moistened with water. It is a symbol of perpetuity and immortality.

From these ideas we can see that each of us has the personal responsibility to engage with our I Am and through this process awaken the presence of Christ within us. This is a personal inner process, not a 'religious' thing spoken of misleadingly in churches today. Those who work on this process shine; they reveal the glory, *doxa*, of the amaranth.

Understanding the idea of eternity comes into these considerations. If we can free ourselves from the birth and death of this life, and have a true experience of having lived previous lives, as well as preparing for future lives, we can experience eternity. It is similar to deciding what to do today that will have an effect on tomorrow, and seeing that what happens today is the result of what took place yesterday.

In this way we can free ourselves, for example, from *"shameful gain"*, *aischrokerdos*, which means greedy. Greed, selfishness, comes from a place which has no connection with the I Am. Greed is an important impulse within us which we should become aware of but not express. It has an awakening energy; as soon as we become aware of it rising up within us we can use the force behind it to become eager, *prothymos*, willing. It is through our will that we can convert the lower impulses to the higher, as Peter says, *"not by constraint but willingly, not for shameful gain but eagerly, not as domineering over those in your charge but being examples to the flock."*

From these ideas we can understand that we are working towards being *"a partaker in the glory that is to be revealed."* As we have considered, this glory involves the raising of our astral being from its instinctive impulses. At the same time, using the energy behind these instinctive impulses to express our highest potential, that is the purpose of our earthly astral expression. Then we will wear "the unfading crown of glory." Then we will stand in eternity and understand the purpose of every event in our lives.

Likewise you that are younger be subject to the elders. Clothe yourselves, all of you, with humility toward one another, for "God opposes the proud, but gives grace to the humble." Humble yourselves therefore under the mighty hand of God, that in due time he may exalt you. Cast all your anxieties on him, for he cares about you. Be sober, be watchful. Your adversary the devil prowls around like a roaring lion, seeking some one to devour. Resist him, firm in your faith, knowing that the same experience of suffering is required of your brotherhood throughout the world. I Peter 5:5-9

Peter now addresses the younger, *neos*, those who are recently born, the ones who are new. He is, of course, addressing those who are giving birth to their spiritual being on the earth. As we stop focusing on our physical life and become conscious of our spiritual being, there are some aspects of which we must become aware. As our spiritual aspects are born, our consciousness of them can be compared to a baby whose movements are awkward and difficult to control.

Even though we may be aware of all the spiritual aspects of our being, often, if we are honest, it is mostly on a theoretical level. This is a start, but we mustn't remain at the baby stage. We must master our movements and increase our conscious awareness if we are to mature as human beings. We can only do this if we experience on some level all the elements of our being. Peter is pointing out the watch-points of this process.

The following words of Rudolf Steiner explain very clearly

the elements of our being that we are becoming aware of.

"What is meant by, "The human being is undergoing development?" Again it is necessary to refer to the being of man. The physical body is only a part of the human entity. This he has in common with all lifeless nature. But he has as second member the etheric or life body, which he has in common only with what is life-imbued. This member wages a continuing battle against everything that would destroy the physical body. Were the etheric body to withdraw from the physical body, in that moment the physical body would become a corpse. The third member is the astral body, which he has in common with animals, the bearer of desires and sorrow, of every feeling and representation, of joy and pain, the so-called consciousness body. The fourth part is his I, the central point of his being, that makes of him the crown of creation. The I transforms the three bodies through development out of the central point of the human being.

Let us consider an uneducated savage, an average man, or a highly educated idealist. The savage is still slave to his passions. The average man refines his urges. He denies himself the satisfaction of certain urges and sets in their place legal concepts or high religious ideals, that is, he remodels his astral body from out his I. As a result the astral body now has two members. The one still has the form that exists in the savage, but the other part has been transformed into Spirit Self or Manas. Through impressions from art or great impressions from founders of religion man works on his ether body and creates Buddhi or Life Spirit. The physical body also can be transformed into Atma, Spirit Man, if a person devotes himself to the practice of certain spiritual-scientific exercises. Thus, the human being works unconsciously or consciously on his three bodies." Rudolf Steiner, Illusory Illness and the Feverish Pursuit of Health, 5 December 1907

When we work unconsciously on these bodies, egotism can arise, which is why Peter stresses the need for humility. Humility *tapeinophrosyne* from *tapeinos*, means not rising far from the ground. At the base of this word is *phren*, one meaning of which is the faculty of perceiving and judging. This gives us a broader understanding of humility. It is not self-effacement; it is about confident judgment expressed by our spiritual being. We must clothe ourselves in this humility, and the word clothe, *enkomboomai*, means a knot or band by which two things are fastened together. We must fasten our physical and spiritual beings together.

What is not always clear is that during this process anxieties arise. We see the rise of anxiety everywhere in the world today. Anxiety is the opposite of the word clothe - the fastening of two things together. Anxieties, *merimna*, meaning care comes from the word *merizo*, which means to divide into parts, cut into pieces, through the idea of distraction.

Peter says that we avoid anxiety by being sober, *nephron*, which means to be calm and collected in spirit, to be temperate, circumspect. He also says that at the same time we should be watchful, *gregoreuo*, which means to give strict attention to, be cautious and active, and comes from *egeiro*, which means to arouse, cause to rise up. This describes the ultimate way of awakening to our spiritual being. So there are parts of us that need not rise far from the ground, and parts that must rise up.

As we go through this process, Peter says, *"Your adversary the devil prowls around like a roaring lion, seeking some one to devour."* Adversary, *antidikos*, means opponent, and comes from the word *dike*, meaning right, just, as in justice meaning balance as we balance the weights on a scale.

We must resist this adversary, and by engaging in the process of resisting through balance we are strengthened. The word resist, *anthistemi*, means to set one's self against, to withstand, and comes from *histemi* meaning to cause or make to stand. As previously mentioned, it is the I Am which gives us the ability to stand on two feet, an ability that sets us apart from all other forms of life on the earth as described in the Rudolf Steiner quote above.

Then we are firm in our faith, *pistis*, which means insightful knowledge not a substitute for knowledge. Then, *"knowing that the same experience of suffering is required"* where knowing, *eido*, means to see, to perceive, discern, or to discover our destiny. This is the true meaning of suffering and it is required of the brotherhood of which we are becoming a part.

And after you have suffered a little while, the God of all grace, who has called you to his eternal glory in Christ, will himself restore, establish, and strengthen you. To him be the dominion for ever and ever. Amen. By Silva'nus, a faithful brother as I regard him, I have written briefly to you, exhorting and declaring that this is the true grace of God; stand fast in it. She who is at Babylon, who is likewise chosen, sends you greetings; and so does my son Mark. Greet one another with the kiss of love. Peace to all of you that are in Christ. I Peter 5:10-14

Peter finishes his first letter with a powerful blessing to sustain us in our work. He reminds us that we will only suffer for a little while, *oligos*, which means a short time and with a slight degree of intensity. It is good to be reminded of the fact that Jesus received into himself the Christ Spirit for all of us. We don't have to go through what he went through but we do have to experience the intensity of it - briefly, as Peter is now reminding us. The way we are able to experience this suffering is through our I Am. In fact, in this way our connection with our I Am, which is the purpose of the crucifixion, is revealed to us.

Then the God of all grace, *charis*, which means to see the pure foundation of everything, which makes us graceful, calls us to experience eternal glory in Christ. We can only experience this if we are transforming our astral from its earthly character to its spiritual purity. Glory is mentioned often in these letters which points to its importance. As glory manifests in our being we begin to shine like a star. This is the glory of the self-born, the *monogenes*, which St John mentions at the end of his Prologue (John 1:1-14).

Through the firsthand experience of suffering, however briefly, we send a signal to the God of all Grace to *"restore, establish, and strengthen"* us. Restore, *katartizo* means to repair, to mend, to make us what we ought to be. Establish, *sterizo,* means to strengthen us and make us firm and stable. *Sterizo* is a derivative of *histemi*, which means to cause or make to stand - and as previously noted it is through our I-being that we have the ability to stand. Strengthen *sthenoo,* essentially means strong in one's soul. Only when we are strong in our soul can we integrate and activate our I Am.

The final words of the blessing are, *"To him be the dominion for ever and ever, Amen."* It is easy to pass over these simple words yet they contain important ideas which can sustain us as we participate in the development these Seven Letters are guiding us through.

It is easy to consider that *"him"* means *"the God of all grace"* but it could also mean those of us who are committed to the work and have the experiences Peter mentions. The word dominion is significant. Dominion in Greek is *kratos* which means power, might. Dominion also refers to the beings of the Spiritual Hierarchy above man whose task it is to keep the Universe in balance. They are continually rebalancing the effects of our lack of understanding of who we are and what our purpose is.

Sergei Prokofieff, in his book, The Heavenly Sophia, spoke of the work of the Dominions or Kyriotetes, quoting words of Rudolf Steiner - see page 35f. The Kyriotetes, in complete devotion immerse themselves in "the impulse to sacrifice something to the new world that is arising, to endow it with the sacrificial outpouring of part of their own beings. And what they thus give to the world can be defined as grace, as 'the bestowing, grace-endowed virtue of true giving' (quoting Steiner)." This is an eternal process, with no beginning or end. Amen - So be it.

The final blessing can be read as is, although we shouldn't overlook the names Peter introduces: Babylon and Mark. Babylon means confusion and Mark means defense. We experience confusion as we develop spiritually, and it is our basic astral that is inclined to be defensive. If we can identify these in our development we will know *"that this is the true grace of God; stand fast in it."* Again the mention of standing directs our attention to our I Am.

Finally, *"Greet one another with the kiss of love. Peace to all of you that are in Christ."* Greet, *aspazomai*, means to draw to one's self. This is an intimate experience unlike the greetings we speak mindlessly today when we say, "How are you?" Also, Peter is saying that when we greet 'one another' *allelon*, it is mutually and reciprocally. We do this with the kiss of love. Kiss is *philema* which means fraternal affection and the kiss is a holy kiss of love, *agape*, the highest love.

"Peace to all of you that are in Christ." Peace, *eirene*, is the experience of inner peace regardless of what takes place around us. When our I Am is active in our soul, and the Christ Spirit begins to awaken, peace is a natural state of being. Then we will truly shine through the glory, the *doxa*, that we ourselves have created.

"Peace to all of you that are in Christ."

ABOUT THE AUTHOR

Kristina Kaine has worked with people all her life: during her early career in medical sales and staff recruitment, and since 1987 in her own business which matches people in business partnerships. Through this rich interaction with people, Kristina has observed the struggle for self identity from many angles.

She was awakened to the ideas of Rudolf Steiner by Rev Mario Schoenmaker, attending all of Schoenmaker's lectures for 14 years. After Schoenmaker's death in 1997, Kristina realised the need to explain the knowledge of the threefold human being in simple terms that could be applied easily in daily life. She has set this out in her book, 'I Connecting : the Soul's Quest', which was published in 2007 by Robert Sardello through Goldenstone Press. It is not unusual for Kristina to receive comments about her book like this: "It seems like a very lucid treatment, like looking through a clear glass window through which one can discover and recognize the landscape of the soul."

Since 2003 Kristina has written weekly reflections which apply this knowledge of the threefold human being to Bible texts. This is not done in the context of any particular religious beliefs but from a broader perspective that all religions could apply. These reflections are distributed by email and are read worldwide. They are available as Kindle ebooks and paperback through Amazon.

Kristina is also a blogger, on Face Book, on her own sites.

www.ingramcontent.com/pod-product-compliance
Lightning Source LLC
Chambersburg PA
CBHW051344040426
42453CB00007B/395